"It is indisputable that people want to interact with people they like. It makes sense, therefore, to like and be liked by as many people as possible. Dr. Kirschner's book, *How to Click with People*, is an insightful, rewarding, and productive way to create rapport with a large number of people."

—Dr. Tony Alessandra,
author of *The Platinum Rule* and *Charisma*

"This compelling look at clicking with people and building the personal side of business will help readers build connections quickly, develop stronger partnerships and teams, and have a higher quality exchange of ideas and information. This book will find use in the hands of any serious business professional with the desire to be proactive in all of their relationships."

—Andrea Sittig-Rolf, author of *Power Referrals*

"As a bestselling author, I receive lots of manuscripts for new books, most of which I view without high expectations. This book is different, though. It is very readable and filled with story after story of how a minor adjustment on your part can reap major rewards in dealing with the world's most challenging people and situations. So if you are a negotiator, a salesperson, a manager, coach, or parent, you will love this book!"

—Jim Cathcart,
author of *The Eight Competencies of Relationship Selling*

"Anyone who intends to lead in this increasingly connected world must master the art of building and developing offline relationships. Dr. Rick Kirschner's engaging book, *How to Click with People*, provides the essential set of people skills to achieve this necessary result."

—Rob Cross, professor of management,
University of Virginia,
and coauthor of *Driving Results Through Social Networks*

"What would your life be like if you clicked with people 50 percent more of the time or 100 percent or even 500 percent? Who would you know? How would your career change? What would your personal life be like? How could you better help others? With Dr. Kirschner's new book you'll learn how to authentically click with more people more of the time and do so in a way that is true and totally you!"

—Vince Thompson, author of *Ignited*

"As our world becomes more connected through social networking, the ability to create a deeper connection or, as Rick explains, *click* on a richer, more meaningful level is becoming a lost art. Whether at home or in the office, *How to Click with People* provides practical, worthwhile solutions so that you can make the impact you want in every conversation and interaction you have, regardless of the type of person you encounter. Discover what the best communicators do so that you can create more satisfaction, fulfillment, and success in your life."

—Keith Rosen,
    author of *Coaching Salespeople into Sales Champions*

"*How to Click with People* is a thoroughly enjoyable tour through the art and science of why and how we resonate with each other. In this age of cascading connectivity and intimacy, a book such as this could not have arrived at a more auspicious time, and Dr. Rick Kirschner is perhaps the only person who could have written it. It will refine your entrepreneurial skills, improve your professional communications and help you to become an attentive, more engaging friend. Highly recommended."

—Dr. Peter D'Adamo,
    bestselling author of *Eat Right 4 Your Type*

"We've all been there. You enter the room and you're immediately drawn to someone, or perhaps repulsed. It's an innate response, internal and subconscious. It's not just about how they look or act, but about how they *'click.'* Dr. Kirschner's latest book describes this mysterious ability to connect with others. He explains how to discover it within yourself and how to create that ability if you don't already have it. It's a must-read for anyone who deals with people at work, though socially it is almost as important.

 —Jon Peters, CEO of AthenaOnline and
  president of the Institute for Management Studies

"Kirschner presents a useful (and usable) model for understanding how to connect with people. His organized approach and clear writing provide an orderly framework for analyzing your communications with others and adjusting your responses. While his ideas seem so logical, these insights aren't common sense. This book is a methodology for building bridges with people of all types."

 —Cary Gutbezahl, MD,
  president and CEO of Compass Clinical Consulting

HOW TO
CLICK
WITH
PEOPLE

HOW TO CLICK WITH PEOPLE

THE SECRET TO BETTER RELATIONSHIPS IN BUSINESS AND IN LIFE

Dr. Rick Kirschner

HYPERION

NEW YORK

Library of Congress
Cataloging-in-Publication Data has been applied
for.

ISBN 978-1-4013-2320-2

Hyperion books are available for
special promotions, premiums, or
corporate training. For details contact
the HarperCollins Special Markets
Department in the New York office at
212-207-7528, fax 212-207-7222, or
e-mail spsales@harpercollins.com.

Book design by Karen Minster

FIRST EDITION

10   9   8   7   6   5   4   3   2   1

THIS LABEL APPLIES TO TEXT STOCK

We try to produce the most beautiful books
possible, and we are also extremely concerned
about the impact of our
manufacturing process on the forests of the
world and the environment as a whole.
Accordingly, we've made sure that all of the
paper we use has been certified as coming
from forests that are managed to ensure the
protection of the people and wildlife
dependent upon them.

TO GOOD PEOPLE EVERYWHERE
WHO CARE, CONNECT, AND WORK EACH DAY
FOR A BETTER TOMORROW.

CONTENTS

ACKNOWLEDGMENTS

First a big thank you to Martha and Peter D'Adamo, who connected me with my wonderful agent, Janis Vallely. Much appreciation to Janis, who clicked with the idea for the book, and helped so expertly to bring it to life. Thanks also to Colleen Kapklein for her insightful editing, help in developing the framework, and ability to find just the right words to express my ideas; to Kate Griffin, who patiently contributed suggestions that have made the book stronger and more valuable to readers; to my good friend Hal Dresner, for his intelligence, wit, and many useful suggestions along the way.

I'm deeply grateful to my wife, Lindea, whose steady spirit, patience, and love of community inspired me throughout; my daughter, mother, father, and siblings, whose relentless confidence in me keeps the wind in my sails; to Jon Peters for his friendship and support; to the helpful program chairs at the Institute for Management Studies for their permission and assistance in developing different portions of this material; to my cat, Rollie, whose playful companionship made the writing more enjoyable. Thanks also to the many people who contributed stories and examples, or tested the reliability of this work.

All together, their enthusiastic belief in this project gives me a persistent hope that we can indeed make the world a better place through engagement with each other and participation in ever expanding networks and communities.

RICK KIRSCHNER
ASHLAND, OREGON

HOW TO
CLICK
WITH
PEOPLE

INTRODUCTION

SOME PEOPLE, YOU JUST CLICK WITH. THE CONNECTION IS quick and easy. They get you, you get them. Communication flows. You could tell them anything, and they'd know just what you mean. You feel seen, heard, and understood. You feel accepted and appreciated for who you really are. And all because you've clicked.

Click. It's that state of mind, that sense of being where everything falls into place. When you click, you gain a new perspective through the worldview of another person. You work better with others and get better results. You develop stronger partnerships and teams. You have a higher quality exchange of ideas and information, resolve interpersonal problems, and play a bigger part in what goes on around you. Best of all, you build real relationships, the kind that last a lifetime.

Chances are you think of click as an instantaneous thing. It either happens or it doesn't. People either get you or they don't. There are a handful of people in this world you click with—and then there's everybody else. Whether you love them or hate them, you're just not ever going to really be in that groove.

You're wrong.

You can learn to click. You can make click happen. Click is a skill like riding a bike or fixing a car, and as a skill, it can be learned.

I've been teaching persuasion, conflict resolution, and relationship skills for close to three decades, and this work has taken me all over the world. I've helped people learn to deal with difficult behavior in coworkers, bosses, and even relatives by teaching them to sort out their own sense of purpose and make fundamental changes in their habits. My clients want to make a meaningful difference in their lives, and I've helped them to find the motivation and approach to accomplish just that. And all of this work is based on the idea that if people are going to get along with each other and get things done together, they first have to click.

Most of what you need to know about success in life is personal in nature. I've learned, through my own experience and that of the people I've worked with, that all of us need one another to have fulfilling work, successful careers, and meaningful lives. Regardless of your cultural background, your age group, or your social status, your need to get along with people is fundamental to your happiness and success. No matter how much technical skill you have in your particular field of expertise, no matter how smart you are, how capable or gifted, if you don't know how to get along with people, you're not going to be successful.

> Your skill with other people is key to your success.

Whether the times are great, or the economy is in the tank, the people who do the best, who prosper and advance, are those who know how to connect with other people in a meaningful way. In other words, those who know how to click.

That's where this book comes in. This book will teach you how to click, to build connections quickly, and then develop them as deeply as you desire. It's just a matter of knowing what to do, why to do it, and how to do it.

In the first half of this book, you will learn how to get people to get you, and how to get them too. Chapter 1 introduces the basic click you can make with anyone at any time. Chapter 2 looks at what makes a person "clickable"—what makes it easy to click with someone—and how to develop that in yourself. Chapter 3 explores the role of listening in drawing people to you.

The next three chapters are about three major "clickable" areas (communication style, motivation, and values) that allow for deeper and closer connections between people.

The following two chapters provide solutions to common trouble spots in clicking: not meeting face-to-face and interacting with difficult people. Chapter 7 discusses how to click effectively via phones, e-mail, and social networking, and Chapter 8 demonstrates how to click with even pushy, critical, negative, unreliable, or sarcastic people.

The second half of the book explores how to get people to get your ideas. Chapter 9 covers "the click zone"—and how (and why) to get into it any time you want to get others onboard with an idea or task. Chapters 10 and 11 show how to present ideas so they appeal to both the head and the heart, and connect with the way people think and feel.

Chapter 12 reveals all the most common stumbling blocks that prevent ideas from clicking—and how to avoid or recover from them. Chapter 13 looks at clicking with groups of people, and creating click within groups. And the final chapter puts all the pieces together to examine "Why We Click."

SUGGESTIONS ON HOW TO USE THIS BOOK

Read It Through

Read the book once, beginning to end. Be open to the ideas and imagine the possibilities. Consider taking a second pass through the book revisiting the material most applicable to you. If any of the ideas seem familiar, but you're not yet acting on what you know, let each lesson remind you to do in the real world what you've only imagined in the past.

Try It Out

Apply every lesson that interests you to at least one person, at least two times. The more you test an idea, the more you understand how it works and how to work with it.

Use It as a Reference

Once you know where everything is in the book, you can find the ideas that you need when you need them, and use them to connect with people in almost any situation. You'll find additional help along the way about where and when a particular lesson would be most valuable to you.

Partner Up

Find someone you already click with and bring him along with you. Read together. Listen together. Talk together. Click together.

Working with a reliable partner in the process of learning will always work better than working alone.

Keep Going

Click into the online opportunities at TheArtofChange.com/ Click. And follow my blog at www.theartofchange.com. These materials can be an ongoing resource for you as you continue to click with the people around you.

CHAPTER 1

The Basic Click

The Power of Resonance

Clicking happens in many ways but at its most basic level, it's all about tapping into the profound power of resonance.

Resonance occurs when vibrating objects respond to other vibrations or frequencies that approximate their natural rate. Resonance makes many things possible: music, radio, TV—and the click.

We've all experienced the power of resonance. When we dance, we can feel a connection to our partner—a sort of synchronicity. When we sing together in harmony, our voices resonate in the same frequency. The effect can touch us, move us, make us well up with tears, or move us to the beat. When we are so in sync that we can practically complete each other's sentences, we've tapped into the power of resonance. And when we've tapped into the power of resonance, we've clicked.

Patterns of Similarity

When meeting someone for the first time, we all make a basic decision, and make it rather quickly: *Is this person similar to me, or not?* Without some pattern of similarity to hold us together, there's no resonance—that means no trust, no cooperation, no benefit of the doubt—and no click. The more essential the pattern, the deeper the click with a person who shares that pattern.

The most obvious patterns of similarity are in the foundational stuff of life, like our needs, motivations, and values. People form organizations around their shared values and work with great diligence to effect the world based on those values.

> If my values are similar to yours, you and I detect that pattern of resonance and begin to share an orbit.

We click when we have a shared culture or tradition. If you and I come from a similar background, which can be heard in the resonance of our accents and colloquialisms, we detect the pattern and our sense of connection grows. People who have served in the military, or done some other form of national service, immediately resonate with others who reveal the same experience in their past. People who have gone through tragedy and triumph together find resonance in the memories of it. They form a bond that those who were not there never quite understand.

We are drawn to the similar because it is familiar and we are comfortable with it.

Blending

This resonance of similar patterns happens naturally when we are already on common ground with someone—with people we care deeply about, or are really interested in, or share significant background or experiences with. But creating it is a skill anyone can acquire. Rather than common ground creating the resonance, consciously invoking the patterns of similarity and resonance can create the common ground. Creating those patterns of similarity is called *blending*, and it is one of the most basic ways to create click.

Blending is all about reducing the differences between yourself and someone else to create a resonant pattern of similarity. This doesn't mean you have to become the same, or pretend to be the same, to create click. But you want to shine the brightest light on the commonalities. Highlighted against a backdrop of similarity, differences become points of interest rather than conflict.

Blending can occur in a lot of different forms, including verbal and nonverbal patterns, communication style, motivation, and values, as explored later in this chapter.

> Blending happens when you notice what's going on and signal a corresponding pattern of similarity.

Click Through Blending

The good news is that you already know how to blend. You do it all the time with the people you resonate with naturally. Now it's time to start observing yourself and others, and using this innate behavioral ability intentionally. You can call on this skill whenever you need or want to create a basic click. All you have to do is pay attention to what people reveal about themselves and align yourself with them. Notice their behavior, their words, their actions, and their stories. If, for example, the other person speaks rapidly, then you speak rapidly. If he gestures a lot, you gesture a lot. If she tends not to look at anyone straight on, you avoid direct or prolonged eye contact too. Blending happens when you notice what's going on and signal a corresponding pattern of similarity.

Remember, you're not trying to copy the other person, as that would quickly become quite boring, and, frankly, unsettling. But you do want to complement and resonate with the person you're with. You can't initiate blending—you can only blend in response to what someone else says or does.

Nonverbal Blending

Many of the most important ways to blend are nonverbal. That's because many of the most important things we communicate are nonverbal. A lot of how we make sense of what other people say is not about what they actually say, but rather how the person looks when delivering the message. In other words, it's not what you say, it's how you say it.

Years ago, I stopped for coffee at a convenience store. The clerk behind the counter was unfriendly and, despite the scowl on his face, I smiled at him. He looked away. When I asked him where the coffee was, he simply pointed to a corner and barked, "Over there!"

I found the coffee, but there wasn't any creamer in sight— only that powdered kind that came in the packets.

"I really dislike nondairy creamer. How about you?" I asked him, hoping to gain some agreement.

"I like it just fine," he said with a snarl.

I asked the clerk for something else, but he was, and this is stating it mildly, unhelpful. "Do you have any milk, cream, or half-and-half? You know, something from a cow?" I inquired playfully.

His response was an aggressive, "No."

Stubborn by nature, I kept pushing. In the corner there was a bin of ice cream, so I asked, "May I have a spoonful of ice cream in my coffee? Might help take the edge off."

He said, "No," and I did not doubt him.

It wasn't until I saw his eyes roll that I realized my body language was saying it all wrong. He wasn't holding coffee or anything else in his hand. He wasn't smiling. He wasn't being playful. And though my intentions were good, I realized that my behavior gave him the impression that I neither liked nor cared about him; as far as he was concerned, I was nothing like him.

So I set down my coffee and matched his posture. I folded my arms across my chest, lowered my head, and I asked him point blank, "Is this something I did, or are you just having a rough day?"

And just like that, he began telling me what was on his mind.

"The night shift left me such a mess! I was cleaning the store for hours this morning; my back is killing me." He paused, relaxed his posture a bit, and finally asked me, "What flavor?" Click!

Blending signals to another person that you are on her side, with her instead of against her, that you are like her in some obvious or subtle way. What's more, blending increases the likelihood of cooperation while reducing the chance for conflict.

• Body Language

Physical blending increases the likelihood of cooperation. By matching your posture to another person's, you jump-start the pattern of resonance. If he's standing and you're sitting, stand up to talk with him. If she's sitting and you're standing, pull up a chair. If he's tapping his pen, you can tap your toe. You'll be complementing not just his body language, but his energy and comfort level as well.

• Personal Space

Most people like to be surrounded by a two- to three-foot bubble, but some people take up a lot of space, and others only a little.

When approaching someone, see how much personal space she tends to surround herself with. If someone moves into your personal space, that's a clue his zone is on the small side. If she pulls back, you know she prefers more space. Be observant and keep your distance, and she'll be comfortable enough to click.

Over the years, Allan had proven himself to be one of the more successful branch managers in his company. Whether it was calming Cheryl down after a frustrating meeting with the investors or encouraging Joseph to take on a difficult marketing call because he knew he could stand up to the challenge, Allan understood his employees and how to foster their success. And those employees, in turn, trusted Allan to always have their back.

Sean was one of Allan's most promising salespeople, despite his young age. Within months on the job, he'd claimed his spot as one of the company's top performers but when he suffered his first setback—losing out on a potentially lucrative prospect—he was utterly beside himself. All the time and energy Sean had put into developing the prospect had come to naught, and he could do nothing but pace around his office, shaking his head and tugging at his hair.

Allan spotted this unusual behavior on his way to the break room and began to pace along with Sean. Where at first there had been only one person wearing down the carpet, there were now two. Neither Allan nor Sean said a word, but they both wore inquisitive, baffled expressions. Sean was not alone in his worry.

After a minute, Sean paused and looked at Allan. With desperation in his voice, he cried, "I don't know what went wrong!"

Allan nodded his head. "Yeah, I get that. It's a tough loss, Sean, but you know what? We'll figure it out. Maybe even find an advantage in it."

That was all he said. Sean instantly straightened and smoothed down his hair, as if taking on the confidence of his manager. The conversation that followed was insightful, and with Allan supporting him, Sean was able to work toward solving the problem.

Verbal Blending

Much important information is, of course, communicated verbally, so this is another opportunity for blending. It's not just the words used, however, but also the way they sound:

• Tempo and Volume

Have you ever had somebody shout at you from three inches away or tried to decipher the words of someone who is mumbling? It's frustrating, to say the least. Just as complementing body language is important in sending the right signals, matching the speed and volume at which someone is speaking is imperative in reaching that click. The mumbler doesn't know how hard it is for you to hear him, but if you speak to him in a similar manner, he'll find it difficult to understand you. Chances are, he'll ask you to speak up. All that's left is to say, "I know! I can't hear you in here either!" You both may have to laugh off the situation, but you'll be able to hear one another from then on.

• Time and Space

Consider how people reference time when they talk. Regardless of when an event actually takes place, some prefer to speak in the past tense, some in the future tense, and some in the here and now.

Consider the following.

At lunch one day, Carlo shared a story about the evening when his partner, Sharon, first met her future employer. When explaining the details, he might have referred to the event in the past tense, saying, "Sharon actually met him at McSorley's after the NCAA tournament." If you were listening, you could have replied with a similar verb tense by asking, "Who did she meet, again?" Likewise, if Carlo were fond of telling stories in the present tense he would have commented in the following manner: "Sharon is at McSorley's watching the NCAA tournament game when she meets him." You could have replied in the present, even though the event was in the past. "Who is she meeting?" It's a subtle way to blend, but it's powerful.

Her: I *was* worried you would miss the meeting.

You: I know you *were*.

Her: But I *am* so looking forward to it.

You: So *am* I.

Her: Now that we're here, what *will* we do first?

You: Let's start with whatever you *will* enjoy most.

Blending doesn't require much effort. It's simple, really, and a little goes a long way. Whether it's posture, gestures, tone, tense, or space, find something, anything, that you can blend with, so you can create the patterns of similarity all humans are wired to respond positively to. You can get in sync with anyone that way, tapping the power of resonance, creating click—and the connection, pleasure, and opportunities that go with it—wherever you go.

CHAPTER 2

Clickability— What Is It and Who Has It?

Be Clear About What You Care About, and Why

People who live with passion find it easier to click with others. Knowing what you really care about, and why, lets you tap into your passion. That internal fire energizes you. It's your energy that draws people to you—it's a click magnet!

When you have the energy to act as if you are always in the right place at the right time, no matter who's around or what's going on, you're showing your clickability. When you have energy to spare, you don't just walk into a room, you make an entrance. You look around, make eye contact, move just a little quicker than everyone else. When you extend your hand, you reach out with confidence and determination. Caring—and knowing what you care about and why—gives you the energy to make connections.

Consider Darla. A part-time student and a full-time employee, she was lucky to get five minutes to herself each day. The stress had been wearing on her for a while, but eventually it began to catch up with her. Exhausted, Darla dragged herself to work every day, often having mismatched her outfit and forgetting to bring along lunch. When she had an opportunity to present her ideas at work, she was too tired to act in her own interest. There was always another pressing issue—a term paper, the dry cleaning, her canary's veterinary bill. Her low energy became an excuse to shut down rather than contribute.

One morning, Darla caught a glimpse of herself in the mirror on her way to work. She was shocked for a moment, unable to recognize the person she saw in the reflection. This wasn't like her—but what had led her down this spiral? She asked herself a few basic questions: "Why should I care about me, even when others don't? Why should I care about the people I meet, even when they are difficult or annoying? Why should I care about how I respond to this day's challenges and opportunities?"

Darla knew she had cared at one point—before all the minutiae of life got in the way. She used to be motivated to develop strategies and deal with all kinds of behaviors. She loved working with people and seeing the positive results of her hard work and efforts. Somewhere along the line, she'd let herself lose sight of what was important—but that had to change. Instead of waiting for her circumstances to change favorably, she would have to make the choice to shape her own circumstances.

To boost her energy, Darla budgeted time for a little peace and quiet every morning wherein she could plan her entire day, including the breaks she would need to recharge her batteries.

The change was small, superficial at first. By simply putting an extra few minutes into getting ready in the morning, she already felt more confident about herself by the time she got to work each day. One small alteration gave way to another and another.

Within a short amount of time, she had bounced back from her slump and had more energy than ever before. She had the time to not only take care of herself, but to reach out, help others, and build the relationships she wanted to. Whenever she walked into a room from then on, everyone noticed. The people around her can't help but respond when she is around.

You don't have to be manic about connecting with others. If you can cultivate your appreciation for and curiosity about the differences between people, you will find that your natural energy, your innate clickability, grows.

Take Responsibility for the Way You Relate to Others

For the sake of this chapter, I'm going to use "responsibility" to refer to the ability to *respond* adequately and wisely to a situation, rather than just *reacting* to it. Responding rather than reacting isn't nearly as difficult as you may think. Simply notice what is happening, connect yourself to it instead of fighting it or withdrawing from it, then find a way to learn from it, leverage it, or leave it behind. When you're in charge of yourself, you know this is your choice. You realize that your greatest leverage in life is your response to what the moment brings.

> Your greatest leverage in life is your response to
> what the moment brings.

The more of your past relationships you resolve, the less of them you carry around. Cleaning up the past is a powerful key to better results with people in the present. Taking charge of yourself takes you beyond reactions to others, so that you can be responsive to them instead. Bear in mind that responsibility isn't about blaming, it's about choosing.

The person in charge of herself can associate tomorrow's consequences with today's choices and today's consequences with yesterday's choices.

For years, Denise had the luxury of working for a female-dominated company, so when she found out her new boss was a man, she wasn't happy about it. If there was one thing she couldn't stand, it was a man in a position of authority. If it wasn't his misogynistic snarls or his sexist predispositions, he would refuse to green-light her project and he was always so full of himself. Sure enough, during their initial meeting, Denise and Richard clashed.

Richard was very direct. "I've already outlined the plans for our product launch," he said, providing a four-color packet for everyone in the meeting.

Denise was irritated that, once again, a man had overshadowed her opportunity to share ideas, and she wasted no time telling him so before he even finished his presentation. Richard acknowledged her input, but insisted on his plan. When he repeated his intentions, Denise lost her temper. Richard, in defending himself, did not react well.

Onlookers at the meeting would have agreed that this was a familiar pattern. After Richard's presentation, one of Denise's colleagues came to her desk to ask her about what had happened. Richard was new, and adjusting to his methods would be difficult, she reassured Denise, but he was their superior and he had to be treated with some level of respect. "And besides," Denise's colleague continued, "this isn't the first time it's happened. What about the supervisor at your old job? Or Bob from accounting? And what about that time you nearly gnawed off your marketing professor's head?"

Slowly, it began to occur to Denise what was going on. She didn't appreciate men telling her what to do. And her friend was right—she was being extremely unprofessional with Richard.

Denise chose to learn from her past mistakes and do the hard work within herself she needed to do to move beyond her issues.

She learned to introduce her own ideas or problems by asking for help, insight, or opinion, rather than simply demanding action (and getting angry when she didn't get it). Instead of reacting to her emotions, she learned to take charge of them. She started to respond to behavior, even less-than-desirable behavior, by Richard or another authority figure, in a connected way, using listening and blending skills.

As it turned out, Richard's original plan worked out okay. At the next launch meeting, Denise used her new strategy to suggest some ideas, which Richard was now able to hear— and accept. And Denise could finally hear his suggestions on how the whole team needed to improve, without polarizing his comments or taking affront. Now she treats Richard with respect—and gets respect in return.

It takes a real commitment to work through whatever baggage you're carrying through life, but when you are ready to put it down you'll appreciate right away how much lighter you'll feel.

To increase your sense of ownership over the moments in your life, start by committing to learn from every experience, and prepare yourself before each new one. After an unsatisfying encounter, revisit what happened and figure out what might have worked better for you. If you can't think of anything, find a role model or a friend who knows better than you what to do, and mentally relive the encounter in a new way. And before dealing with anyone or starting a conversation, ask yourself what you want to have happen by the end. You will develop your ability to respond to what the moment brings.

Treat Each Person Equally

Having clickability means treating everyone equally—the way you want to be treated.

We all have needs and wants. No matter how good (or bad) we are at something, there is always someone better (or worse) at it. We've all fallen short, but our failures and disappointments don't make us *less than*—they help us become who we are.

When you are fair-minded and evenhanded, you recognize that everyone is doing the best they know how. You may not have all the answers, but you can safely assume that no one else has all the answers either. Even the simple questions may prove worth your time and consideration.

I've known, interviewed, and worked closely with plenty of successful people. I've met CEOs and presidents, royalty and prodigies. The more successful people are, the *less* likely they are to show off, put on airs, or drop names. They don't waste time trying to impress. They know there is more to gain in life through connection and positive relationship. The same goes for successful mailroom employees, students, and mid-level managers. Life isn't fair, but people almost always prefer fairness from other people. And remember: *All* business is people business.

Be Attentive

When it comes to making people feel special, it's the little things that count the most. Starting with something as simple as a name. Names *matter.* They are handles for identity, for who we are, and how we want to be addressed. You may have met people in your life who took liberties with your name, who assigned you a nickname that didn't fit or that you didn't care for at all, and you didn't like it, did you? Most people don't tell you when they're unhappy with the name you call them, but they are likely to hold it against you. There goes that click.

Notice how people introduce themselves, and let that be your guide in addressing them, at least initially. If you want to switch from a formal name to a more informal one, ask permission. So if you're talking with someone who was introduced to you as Dr. Sam Smart, you can ask, "Dr. Smart, may I call you Sam?" Odds are, in that moment, you will get a satisfying click.

Once you've found a way in, keep the conversation going. So many believe that small talk is cheap, but I've found it can make a big impression. People love to talk about themselves. Being attentive to people means trying to engage people by encouraging them to talk about themselves. Those who don't will try to turn the conversation back to you. In that case, use what you say to bring up material to ask them about. "I've been to Bali, Hong Kong, and Singapore. What about you? Have you ever traveled to Asia?"

The most intimidating aspect of small talk is knowing what, exactly, to talk about. Just remember these four topics, and you'll be fine: Work. Family. Hobbies. Culture.

Most small talk between strangers begins with *work* because most people have plenty to say about what they do in life. They either love it and want to talk about it, or hate it and need to blow off some steam. Either way, someone will have an opinion, and once they feel they can trust you, they'll be more likely to open up.

Family is a more personal topic. Conversations about family with people you don't know have to be casual because family can be a touchy subject with some. Try asking to see photographs or listen for a mention of a spouse or other family member, and use that as a way to get further into conversation. Be attentive and interested in whatever they say about family.

Hobbies are what people do in their spare time. Getting people talking about hobbies can be a lot of fun and a great way to connect with someone. You can learn a lot about someone's strengths just by knowing what it is they like to do. When you get people talking about things they love doing for their own sake, you empower them, which makes for a strong start in building a click.

Culture is a huge opportunity for conversation. Almost everyone reads books, sees movies, watches celebrities, follows a team, and/or has opinions about what goes on in society at large. When you ask people for their opinions on cultural touchstones (the death of a movie star, the latest novel recommended by Oprah, or the latest sporting championship—or scandal), don't be surprised if the floodgates of connection open and a torrent of opinion comes your way.

All you need to start conversations with strangers are a few open-ended questions After a friendly greeting, use conversation-sparking questions such as:

- **Family:**

  "Where are you from originally?"

  "Are you married?"

  "Do you have any kids?"

- **Work:**

  "So, what do you do?"

  "How long have you been doing it?"

  "What do you like about that?"

  "What have you learned from doing it?"

  "What would you change if you could?"

- **Hobbies:**

  "What do you do in your spare time?"

  "What do you like most about it?"

- **Culture:**

  "What do you think about (this movie or that book or the local sports team)?"

  "Do you know of any good restaurants around here?"

You can also try questions about life in general. These kinds of questions are real icebreakers. I've been to parties where the hosts encouraged everyone to talk to someone they didn't know and find out something unique or special about her. Try asking questions like: "If you could go anywhere or do anything, where would you go and what would you do?" "What's the most interesting thing you've ever done?" and "Who was the most interesting person you ever met?" Before long, everyone will be talking to everyone, and real clicking will happen instead of people staying isolated in their cliques.

Everyone has a story to tell. When you get people talking about themselves and their unique experiences, they experience being special around you. I've heard plenty of stories about people who met total strangers, had a brief conversation, and those strangers became important allies, significant connections, and dearest friends.

Try this. When you're sitting next to someone on a plane or a bus or in a restaurant, turn to her, ask permission—"May I ask you something?"—and then ask a few open-ended questions with the potential to reveal something unique about the person.

Maybe she'll shrug you off. But maybe she'll take the bait and tell you something that is unique, special, and even unexpected. And just maybe you will walk away with a great story to tell. And maybe she will too . . . about a total stranger who asked them the most interesting questions.

And if it's you who winds up with an inquisitive seatmate on an airplane, and you don't want to click, give him a reason, any reason, and ask for his understanding. All you have to say is, "Sorry, I just want to be quiet for a while. I have a lot on my mind. I hope you'll understand." Then, even though you're not talking with the person, your considerate response to his attempt to start a conversation is likely to get you a positive silence instead of a hostile neighbor. If you change your mind later in the flight, he'll still be receptive, too.

Third Time's the Charm. People only need two or three examples of you showing an interest in something special to them to decide that you are someone special.

Asking a question to learn more about something a person has said is an easy way to indicate interest. Signaling agreement with something he's said by nodding your head indicates interest. Simply acknowledging that something she's said to you is important to her is a signal of interest. And each time you engage with someone as if he is interesting, you're building his generalization about you. Once your attentiveness puts that generalization in his mind, he'll look for evidence to prove it to himself. And it just takes two or three occasions. *Click.*

How to Convey Personal Warmth

People who know how to connect with others tend to be warmer rather than colder. You can't go wrong being just a little warmer than the people around you (just don't be too intense). If you're not warm enough, you're likely to strike people as remote, standoffish, even arrogant. If you're interacting with a cooler person, your personal warmth is still essential to making a connection, dialed down a bit to keep him comfortable.

There are several ways to convey warmth. Consider how you:

Move. Warmth comes across when your body seems undefended. Maintain a relaxed and open posture, whether you are in a casual setting or a formal one. Face people, but not straight on (at first)—turn toward them at a slight angle. Once they've had a chance to get comfortable with you, move so you interact completely face-to-face.

Welcome people into your personal space. You should invite people into your space rather than invade theirs. When entering a room, survey it before entering. When your eyes land on someone, let your attention linger long enough to let individuals actually notice you noticing them, then smile—and give them a chance to respond in kind. A small smile with a stranger creates warmth, whereas an overpowering smile can intimidate those who feel distant already.

Position yourself. When someone starts to talk with you, take note of how much space she takes up, and respond accordingly. Be aware of her personal space, and move just to the edge of it, but never beyond. When you talk to someone, get close—but not too close. Close enough that if he talks quietly you can hear it—but if he talks loudly it doesn't overwhelm you.

Look at people. No matter how near or far you are, let people see warmth in your eyes. Focus on the person you are interacting with—your gaze should not be scouting around as if for a better opportunity. This doesn't necessarily mean to look her directly in the eye—to some people that can be intimidating. As is often the case, take your cue from the other person—if her eyes are slightly averted, you do the same. If she's gazing steadily at you, you do the same.

Speak. Let people hear the warmth in your voice. Use a friendly and helpful tone in what you say. The best way to sound helpful is to intend to be helpful. The best way to convey warmth with your voice is to relax when you speak. A warm voice is full instead of thin, and is easy on the ears because it sounds re- laxed. Let your shoulders hang easily, instead of throwing them back to hold your chest out. This will send the message that you are interested in the person you are talking with, and interested in what she is saying. The way you talk (not just what you say) should indicate that, whatever your subject, it is something worth hearing, knowing, and understanding.

Attend to people. Hold the other person at the center of your attention. With some people, that means looking into their eyes when they look at you, or for people who don't make eye contact, placing the sound of them in the center of what you hear. Turn your body to face them. Nod your head and make sounds of approval when they talk, so they can see and hear that you are paying attention closely. Any person you talk with should feel like they are the only person in your world in that moment. Many politicians, including Bill Clinton and Barack Obama, are famously good at making a person feel he or she is the most important person in the room—even amid swarming crowds.

When I was a kid growing up in Cincinnati, there was a pop- ular TV show called *The Uncle Al Show*. The host, Al Lewis, played Uncle Al, and his wife, Wanda, played Captain Windy.

One of the two sponsors for his show was a company called Stegner's. Uncle Al would talk about Stegner's chile con carne and, even though I had no idea what chile con carne was, my mouth would start watering. Just the way he said the words let me know this was definitely something I wanted. He wrapped his mouth around the words, he sounded hungry for whatever this product was, and that made it sound delicious. It was like he heated the words in his mouth before letting them out into the world. Warm words are powerful. They draw attention and create excitement. They make you hungry for more.

Some people are born with clickability. But if you happen to be one of the many who wasn't, you can develop as much of it in yourself as you desire. To increase your clickability, you need to know what you care about (and why); take responsibility for your relationships; treat each person as your equal; be attentive and interested in other people's lives; and convey personal warmth.

Then watch your network grow.

CHAPTER 3

A Short Course on Listening

THERE ARE THREE THINGS YOU CAN KNOW ABOUT PEOPLE before they ever say a word:

1. They love to hear themselves talk.
2. They want to be heard and understood.
3. They are drawn to people who listen to them.

When you listen to people talk, you give them the chance to do something they love. When you help people feel heard and understood, they appreciate you for hearing them out. And when you listen well to what others say, they want to be around you. In this way, your influence in their lives will increase.

Now, you may think you're a good listener and perhaps you are. But do you know how to listen for that click?

Listening for the click isn't just listening; it's really *hearing* what people have to say and listening actively for what's really important. The key is to draw people out, to let them know that you are engaged, and that you really want to understand them.

Listen before you talk.

Before you can know what to talk about with someone, you have to listen to him.

Connected Listening

Listening is important in all business—mine is no exception. I try always to keep that in mind, as I did when I received the call from Stan, who was considering hiring me as a business coach. He wanted to hear what I had to say about my services, how I would work with him, and what he could expect.

"I don't even know what to ask about coaching," he admitted. "Maybe you could help me to see what it is you do?"

What he was really asking was whether we would click.

Now, I like talking about myself and my business at least as much as the next person, but instead of talking, what I actually did was listen. Sure, I opened my mouth to let out a few short questions about where he was in his career and relationships, what he hoped to accomplish in his work and in his life, and what he thought about coaching—and yes, I grunted a lot of *uh-huh*'s and *I see*'s and *mm-hmm*'s—but mostly I used my ears and let him do the talking. I learned about the rapid growth of his company and the plateau it had hit. I heard about his new baby and how cute she was. I noted how he described the way he managed his few employees, and listened as he described his role in the company.

In the end, I spoke about myself for only a minute or two. I really didn't have to say much before Stan asked to schedule his first session. By listening rather than talking, and asking the right questions, I got to know Stan well enough that it was easy to click.

Look Like You Understand
Sound Like You Understand

Have you ever tried to tell someone something and she looked or sounded confused while you talked, or began shaking her head in disagreement? Chances are you were so busy trying to figure out what she disagreed with, you were unable to complete your thought. To click—to engage through listening— your behavior has to draw people out. What you want is for them to get past the superficial thoughts and really get down to the heart of the matter.

When speaking with someone, look like you understand, even when you don't. Nod your head when people talk to you as if what they say makes complete sense, even though it may not. Sound like you understand. Utter affirming phrases every once in a while, like *yes, mhmm, I see, oh, uh-huh*, or just grunt affirmatively, as if you know just what they mean. Even if you don't.

Now, you may be worried that you'll mislead the speaker or that you'll have to proceed as if you understand something you don't. Nothing could be further from the truth. You've merely given the speaker a respectful space in which to express himself. You've given him a chance.

Backtracking: Talk Like You Understand

Once you've given the speaker an opportunity to express himself—and have even encouraged him to do so—you'll need to backtrack. By repeating what you've just heard from the other person, you can demonstrate that you're both on the same page. More importantly, backtracking the conversation lets the other person know he's been heard, and that you value what he is saying.

The idea is to repeat the key words, phrases, and ideas you've just heard so as to clarify the information. If someone who is standing on her soapbox declares, "There are simply too many people making too many demands and too little time to address them," you don't need to repeat all of that back. You could simply nod and say, "Mhmm, far too little time to address them."

If you aren't used to this connected way of listening—looking, sounding, and talking like you understand—it may seem a bit awkward at first. But hang tough; you'll be amazed at how quickly you get the hang of it. Backtracking is actually an easier and more effective way to hear and understand someone than trying to guess or, worse, misinterpreting and reacting to what he is saying.

Ask the Right Questions

When the person you're trying to click with has finished making his point, the time has come to ask questions. Your intention is to clarify anything you don't understand. Ask one question at a time, and make sure you pause to listen well to the response. Repeat as needed until you've clarified everything and filled in all the blanks.

Most people don't ask many questions, and when they do, they are often not the right questions. We may be afraid of looking stupid. Or maybe we think asking questions makes us seem weak. Or maybe we just think we're supposed to have all the answers. Since we can think much faster (500 words a minute) than we speak (about 130 words a minute), it's pretty easy for our minds to wander to what we want to say when we ought to be listening.

Good listeners understand the limits of their knowledge. They are not afraid to explore the unknown to build the connection. The key is curiosity. The less you think you know, the more you find out. And the more value you place on what you can learn by listening, the less distracted you'll be with your own thoughts.

The Stupid Question vs. the Dumb Question

Perhaps you've heard it said that "There is no such thing as a stupid question." That's a great guide when it comes to everyone else. When someone asks you a question, no matter how trite, simplistic, or off the point it seems to be, answering that question can be an opportunity to click.

> Questions—the right questions—
> are powerful tools for clicking.

When it comes to what *you* ask, however, there is such a thing as a *dumb* question. Dumb questions fail to take the things people say into account. Dumb questions assume too much and ask too little. If someone tells you "I hate active listening," a dumb question would be "Why don't you give it a chance?"

Questions—the right questions—are powerful tools for clicking. When you ask questions, they should serve an intelligent purpose. You can use them to draw people toward you as well as to set direction and expectation in an interaction. Questions demonstrate empathy, uncover opposition, invite thought, reveal motivation and intent, and get to deeper meaning.

What's more, your questions can be used to inform not just you, but the person who is talking to you. So choose them wisely.

Who? What? Where? When? How?

Start with open-ended questions that begin with the basic five: *who, what, where, when,* and *how.* The great thing about these words is that it's impossible to answer any of them with a yes/no response.

Let's use my pet peeve—active listening—as an example. If you ask me "What do you hate about active listening?" I would tell you, "It seems to require that a person hallucinate freely about another person's meaning." If you asked me "What do you mean by hallucinate freely?" I'd probably tell you that making assumptions and guessing what's going on for people is different than finding out. If you then asked me, "When do you hate it?" I could tell you, "Not always. It's fun when friends do it sometimes. But anytime someone is trying to get to know me, I hate if she starts making assumptions and projecting them on me instead of asking me what I think and hearing it for what it means to me."

You may notice that I haven't included *why* in this list of questions. *Why* is also an open-ended question, but I recommend that you hold off on asking *why* until you've found out who, what, where, when, and how. Most people don't know *what* they're talking about; they're only telling you what's at the surface of their thought. The only way they can answer *why* is to make something up. And that takes you off track! If you can get someone thinking about a topic by engaging her with the basic five questions first, she'll be ready to openly and honestly tell you *why*.

Ask for Relevancy

There are a couple of other questions you can ask too. When people give you two or more ideas that sound unrelated, you can ask for their relevancy.

> The relevancy question: "What does that one idea
> have to do with the other idea?"

This is a great question when talking to someone who sounds confused, and it's the perfect response to a non sequitur. Asking for the relevance or relationship between two ideas takes you out of the position of having to make sense out of nonsense. Instead, the speaker has to clarify what he is trying to say. In other words, it's not your job to figure out what other people mean. Ask them, and let them figure it out.

Introduce Information as a Question

Sometimes the best way to tell someone something is to ask him for his thoughts. He may be more likely to consider what you say that way, in order to answer your question, than he might be if you just stated it flat out.

This is particularly useful when dealing with someone who has expressed an opinion about some limitation. For example, your manager informs everyone in the office about a memo from corporate headquarters in which all unnecessary spending must be eliminated.

"That means no office party for the staff this year. Unfortunately, this is not open for discussion. Sorry," he says to everyone.

It sounds like it's a firm conclusion, yet that little "sorry" at the end implies that you may get some sympathy and might have an opening, *if* you have a better idea.

There are two avenues you could take in this situation.

1. Blend with the manager's positive intent. Tell him "I know how much you care about morale, and it's already been pretty low around here since that last round of budget cuts."
2. Blend with the expression of sympathy.

Tell him: "That's a shame about the office party, because the staff really love it, and it's been great for morale."

Once you've got his attention, ask for his thoughts as you introduce your idea.

"What if we could pay for it without having to involve corporate at all? What would you think about that?"

If you get any interest, even if it's just a confused look, proceed.

"There's been a lot of griping around here about the belt-tightening, and that has a dampening effect on morale. So what if we took advantage of that? What if we were to use the pickle jar approach, where we set a large pickle jar in the corner, and anytime someone complains, she has to put a quarter in it? What if we told people that it's everyone's job to hold each other accountable for this, and at the end of the quarter, whatever is in that jar we use for the party?"

Even though you're asking questions, you've presented an

idea, explained your reason for it, and even described how it works. All that's left for your manager to do is to consider it and respond. If the information is good, or the idea is workable, you'll likely get a positive response. But at the least, you can get him to consider what you have to say.

Ask for Intent

Sometimes when people talk, they give too much information. Instead of you trying to figure out what you've heard, you can simply ask that person her intention. Say, for example, I tell you that I hate active listening. You do your due diligence and find out what I hate about it and so forth, but you still don't quite understand what it means to me. Before the situation becomes any more convoluted, you could ask me, "What is your intent in telling me this?"

I step down from my soapbox and simply reply, "To protect you from a common and counterproductive listening habit that interferes with quality connections."

Now we're both on the same page.

Ask Even if You Already Know

Be wary of believing that you understand anything on the first pass. If you think you know something, you will stop trying to find out anything more. And even if you understand more than you've been told, *ask about it anyway*. If you accept without question the first thing you hear, you pass up an important opportunity not only to confirm or expand your understanding, but also to have the other person feel understood. You lose a chance to click.

Tell Me More

When you find that you don't know what to ask—or you are at a loss for words—simply say, "Tell me more." This is, after all, what you really want in any case. This works particularly well with a person who is verbose. It may seem a little counterintuitive, but the fact is that when you ask someone to "Tell me more," you'll ironically get a much more concise statement of the same information.

Listen for Feelings, Not Just Words

If communication were a strictly logical enterprise, you could take a Sergeant Friday approach: "Just the facts, ma'am." But communication is more than logic. People want to be heard and understood emotionally. Ask enough questions, and what you're hearing will make at least some sense, but all the while, there may be an emotional message underlying the words, a message that comes through in the tone of voice.

People want to be heard and understood
not just logically, but also emotionally.

When a manager says to an employee, "You said you knew how to do that," there's the fact to her statement, and then there's the feeling behind it. The fact of it is that the manager believes that the employee made the claim, "I know how to do it." The emotion behind her statement, however, may carry several messages that can fall anywhere between "You've lied" and "I'm very impressed." Learning to hear both words and feelings is a valuable skill. When the words don't match the feeling, you can ask about the feeling to add meaning to the words. This can reveal some amazingly powerful information that leads to a much deeper click.

A Time and a Place for Connected Listening

Connected listening is a reliable key to getting a click and it is an excellent way to deepen a click. The more you hear, the more you know, and the more you know, the more the person feels heard and understood. Yet not all occasions are conducive to this kind of listening, nor is it necessary all the time. There are a few occasions when connected listening is best.

• When Someone Is Upset

When emotions are running high, it's usually stress that's doing the talking. People in intense emotional states are so wrapped up in themselves that there is no immediate way to connect with them. Helping them pull themselves together is a great opportunity for a click, if you go about it in the right way.

Help them reconnect their brain to their mouths. When you're speaking with someone who's very emotional, it's important to look and sound like her extremely emotional language makes all the sense in the world, even though it may make no sense at all. Once she's able to talk through whatever is bothering her, she'll no longer let emotion do the talking; instead, she'll be talking about emotion. More importantly, though, she'll feel like you understand.

• When You Suspect a Hidden Agenda

When you have a hunch that there's something that someone is not saying, or that someone is withholding important information, connected listening can help you uncover it, reveal it, and deal with it.

One sign that you may not yet have heard *everything* is the use of the minimal expressions of doubt I call hedge words: *maybe, pretty much, almost certain, pretty sure,* and the like. When you hear one of these, you need to gently inquire further:

He says: "And that pretty much covers it. I think you've got just about everything you need to proceed."

You say: "Okay, I've got just about everything I need to proceed. When you say, just about everything, what don't I have?"

You're likely to get a straight answer because he wasn't expecting it, and because you didn't signal him to defend against it. Before you know it, out comes the missing information.

• When Someone Doesn't Know What He Means

Anytime you find yourself talking with someone who doesn't know what she is talking about, you can use connected listening to point out missing information without putting her on the defensive.

She says, "This project will involve numerous operations and procedures by various groups in order to bring the process through to an appropriate result." You say, "The project will involve numerous operations. What operations will be involved?" or "Mhmm. Various groups. Which groups?" By asking for the missing information, you put the person in the position of either filling in the blanks, or arriving at the conclusion that she doesn't know. At that point, you're both in the know and can proceed from there.

• When Dealing with Criticism

When someone is picking at you, finding fault, or otherwise putting you down, it's only natural to want to defend yourself. The problem is that going on the defensive makes you look more guilty than had you said nothing at all. When you defend yourself against criticism, you come off as "protesting too much," as a latter-day Hamlet might have it.

I remember watching exactly that happen on a television reality show, when one of the contestants accused another of being controlling, domineering, and unable to take criticism.

The accused immediately began to defend herself by interrupting and repeating, "I'm not domineering. I can take criticism."

The other contestants gave each other knowing looks. Her behavior seemed to prove the criticism. Smart questions would have served her better, turning the dynamic of the interaction in a more constructive direction. Questions like "Domineering and controlling in what way?" or "What criticism do you want me to take?"

How should you deal with criticism? Change the dynamic from dealing with the criticism to understanding the person offering it. You may learn something useful about yourself or, at least, about interacting with this person.

• When You Want to Persuade

Effective persuasion starts with understanding. It is not about you doing the talking to get your point across; persuasion is more about listening. Let's consider Martin's situation. Having only recently been promoted, Martin was very careful to cover all his tracks. During the preparation for an upcoming presentation, he thought his team had overlooked a key objective from their client, Paws and Rewind Pet Grooming. When he mentioned the discrepancy to Cynthia, the project manager, she looked at him as if he was nuts.

"The meeting is in three days, Martin," she reminded him. "We don't have enough time to reinvent the wheel. The important thing now is to make sure this presentation is ready on time."

That strategy clearly wasn't going to work. Not wanting to have Cynthia on the defensive, Martin changed tactics. Instead of simply pressing his case, he tried instead to understand Cynthia's approach.

"Maybe I've missed something," he said. "Please help me understand how this presentation will meet all the client's needs."

Cynthia sighed. "Martin, I've told you once, I've told you a thousand times. Right now, we just need to make sure it's finished. We'll never get the contract signed without it." The way she saw it, their whole relationship with this client was riding on making the deadline.

Martin heard her overriding concern. He knew that Cynthia would not be able to really hear him if it seemed he was suggesting anything that would threaten to slow their progress to the point where they wouldn't be ready by the appointed day. Wanting to make it clear to her that he had heard and understood her concern, he said, "I know how important this client relationship is and I promise you, we'll be ready on time no matter what. But I'm sure you wouldn't want us to drop this ball any more than they would. So can we review how we will address the concern? And what would happen if we did this instead . . ."

Then, and only then, did Martin lay out his ideas for enhancing the presentation. Reassured that her most pressing concerns were being handled, Cynthia was able to hear Martin's concerns. Then she responded to them on their merits—and got them into the presentation ahead of the big day.

Connected listening lets you hear what makes people who they are. It can get you facts and information that can guide your actions. It can uncover difficulties before they become full-blown problems—and sometimes even solve them without further ado. Listening well is what prepares you to speak well, though you may also find that there's nothing you need to say.

Whenever people talk, what they most want is to be heard and understood. Providing that experience is what really creates the click.

CHAPTER 4

Click in Style

TO BUILD CONNECTION WITH PEOPLE, YOU NEED TO UN-derstand four basic styles of communication: action, accuracy, approval, and appreciation. Each mode reflects the need of the person you're addressing and what he's most likely to respond to. If you're speaking to a person who is after accuracy above all else, you're going to miss the mark if your focus is on praising her, for example. But give her details, lots of carefully considered details, and you'll click right along. For a person craving action, on the other hand, the longer a communication takes, the less satisfying and possibly more irritating it is. Get right to the point and match his "can do" attitude, however, and you'll click.

Identifying an Action-Based Individual

A person using an action-based communication style is verbally direct and goal-focused. She'll talk about *doing* something, or getting things *done*. She'll talk about an objective, or a result, and she'll do it quickly. Movement and momentum have the highest priority, and there will be a clear direction in what she is saying, either toward a desired end or away from a feared result. She is likely to speak in a commanding and authoritative manner, speak quickly, and keep up a brisk pace of conversation. She doesn't do small talk. Her voice is likely louder than normal. She wants her interactions to lead to action.

Action-based communication sounds like:

"Make it happen."

"Get it done."

"Stop beating around the bush."

"Follow through."

When stating an opinion in this style, it sounds like a given, like a matter of fact. *"There are three ways to do this."* You're unlikely to hear a compliment, and it's difficult to use for networking because, where networking is all about personal connections, this style is about impersonal outcomes: short statements and signals of impatience like interruptions, or finger tapping, indicating that there's too much talk and not enough evidence of action. You will hear rapid speech, and words that seek to put the conversation behind you, like okay, and fine, and *I'll get back to you later.*

Action-based communication looks like:

Individuals driven by a need to act will be eager to make eye contact or move into others' personal spaces. They will often move in a straight line, as if to get somewhere in the fewest number of steps.

Action-based communication reads in e-mail:
Messages are extremely brief and may consist of sentence fragments. There will be a notable lack of personal identifiers, for example: "Saw the movie. Didn't get it." "Here's the report. Reply ASAP."

The Action Click

When a person is direct and to the point, your response should also be direct and to the point. Speak assertively. Be matter of fact. Let him hear direction in your words—direction toward a decision, conclusion, opinion, or action.

Helpful Phrases for the Action Click:
    "I want to tell you about . . ." (put a short summary of
       what you're getting at right up front)
    "Here's where I'm going with this . . ."
    "Consider this . . ."
    "You can . . ."
    "Let me get right to the point . . ."
    "Moving right along . . ."
    "What's the bottom line? It's this . . ."
    Want to click? Get to it. The faster things move forward, the better this person will respond to you.

Identifying an
Accuracy-Based Individual

A person using an accuracy-based communication style is also focused on goals, but will pay more attention on the process and the details. Verbally, he is indirect. He speaks slowly and in a restrained manner, offering a lot of particulars, and takes his time getting to the point, if he gets there at all. He may ask a lot of questions to acquire more information and specifics, and make long statements to establish facts and stimulate thinking. You might hear a long-winded explanation that walks you through something already done. He talks about steps and procedure. He is deliberate. He wants to avoid mistakes. He needs more time to address a given subject than people using other styles might. His tone may be flat and systematic. If the communication moves along too quickly, or is too general, it may be difficult for him to maintain interest, so it will be important to be methodical and thorough in your conversations.

Accuracy-based communication sounds like:

"After considering the many variables . . ."

"There are many facts to consider . . ."

"Before proceeding, a careful analysis might yield . . ."

Don't be surprised to hear a counting-off of items, as if reading a checklist. An opinion may sound more like an analysis, and likely it will have no conclusion, but instead end with options. Concerns, when expressed, will highlight missing information, a break in the chain of events, or an erroneous conclusion based on inadequate evidence. An accuracy-oriented individual describes every step and detail beginning to end. It may seem like the person doesn't hear you, because he continues on when you speak as if you didn't say a word.

Accuracy-based communication looks like:
People prone to an accuracy-based style of communication often break eye contact or look away while talking, as if to pay closer attention to their own thought processes rather than being distracted by your responses.

Accuracy-based communication reads in e-mail:
The content will often be composed of several paragraphs and long sentences that say little while saying much. The message may also be filled with statistics and factual references.

The Accuracy Click

Let this person hear that you are paying attention to the details and consider them important. Repeat several of the details she gave you, and offer the details of what you want her to consider. Be somewhat indirect, but be sure to go step by step through whatever you have to say. With someone using this communication style, being impersonal will actually yield a stronger click. Leave out your feelings and hold off on conclusions, and let her hear you think out loud. Your math teacher might call this *showing your work*. Let her hear how you arrive at a conclusion before telling her your conclusion.

Helpful Phrases for the Accuracy Click:

"Something worthy of discussion is . . ."

"It's reasonable to explore the various ways . . ."

"When broken down into its component parts . . ."

"There are a lot of reasons to take into account . . ."

The best way to click with this person is to take your time and get specific. If time is an issue, don't go forward too fast or you might leave them behind. Instead, you can hurry things up by slowing down.

Identifying an Approval-Based Individual

A person using an approval-based communication style is also verbally indirect, but her focus is on people rather than issues. She talks more about *being* than *doing*, and she can tie any subject back to its affect on you or others. She is concerned primarily with other people and how they feel more than her own thoughts, feelings, and opinions. When she speaks, she will be as indirect as possible so as to avoid conflict. She expresses concern for the opinions and feelings of others, and checks in constantly to be sure she gives no offense. She can be helpful, friendly, thoughtful, sensitive to other people's needs, and respectful of their time, because what she wants is to get along with others. She is measured and considerate. She speaks slowly, in soft and caring tones. Her tone may be tentative or deferring. She may be hesitant to ask, or make statements that sound like questions, as if she is running them by you for your opinion. She is likely to qualify what she's saying to make sure it is appropriate. If other people are too abrupt, pushy, or demanding, it's difficult for a person using this style to connect with them. She clicks with people who speak with care and consideration, offering reassurance, and deferring to them.

Approval-based communication sounds like:

"Is this a good time?"

"Is there something you want to tell me . . .?"

"What do you think?"

"I feel like you really are doing a great job."

If the person doesn't have anything nice to say, he'll probably say nothing at all. And if he does say something, expect it to be loaded with cushioning statements and softeners, like "You probably didn't know . . ." and "It's not a big deal or anything but . . ." and "No offense, but I was hoping . . ." Approval-seeking communication also seeks to avoid conflict whenever possible and to minimize misunderstanding by talking indirectly. *"I don't mean to argue, but . . ."* or *"Please don't take this the wrong way, but . . ."*

Expect to be thanked repeatedly for each small offering of assistance. *"Thank you"* and *"That's great, I'm so relieved."* Expect polite communication, and to be treated as if you are important. The approval-seeking communicator may be self-deprecating.

Approval-based communication looks like:
She may wear an out of place smile, offer a hesitant touch, or a tenuous handshake, as if to determine if it will be accepted before fully offered.

Approval-based communication reads in e-mail:
You may find e-mails from her are filled with warm greetings and sign-offs. There may often be references to positive memories scattered throughout and inquiries about personal matters. She may be interested in your feelings and offer long, indirect explanations to avoid even a hint of conflict.

The Approval Click

The key here is to be considerate yourself, and to let the person hear you taking others' thoughts and feelings into account. Be friendly. Speak patiently and with care. Talk about the relationship between the two of you, rather than focusing on her directly.

Helpful Phrases for the Approval Click:

"You and I . . ."

"What do you think we should do?"

"How do you feel about our choices . . . ?"

"Here's what this will mean to us . . ."

"Everyone's on board . . ."

"Do you mind . . . ?"

"Is this a good time . . . ?"

Build a relationship with someone using this style by focusing attention on the relationship, and your relationship to others, within your conversation.

Identifying an Appreciation-Based Individual

A person using an appreciation-based communication style is focused on people as opposed to goals, and on *being* rather than *doing*, but he is verbally direct. He is more aware of—and talks more about—himself. He speaks often of his achievements and accomplishments with energy, enthusiasm, and passion. In conversation, he will use exclamations and personal anecdotes to make his point. He strives to evoke feelings about what he deems important and will be glad to elaborate. The appreciation-seeker is garrulous because it's not about some *thing* in particular—it's about some *one; it's about him.*

If there's a bottom line, he gives it to you up front, then goes on about it with passion. He responds most positively to people speaking equally energetically, even in disagreements. He needs to feel special, and if an interaction fails to give recognition where it is due (or where it is at least desired), he may tune out, put it down, get angry, or walk away.

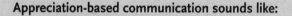

Appreciation-based communication sounds like:

> *"I feel we ought to do this, and I'll tell you why."*
> *"I've given this a lot of thought, because it's important to me..."*
> *"I can see that if I were to do this, I would..."*
> *"I feel strongly about this. I hope you'll listen to me, because I'm sure this is so."*

The voice may even go up in volume to emphasize the person's feelings. Hyperbole might be used to inflate an idea or an opinion in order to draw attention to it. *"I always say..."* or *"Everybody knows..."* The person who engages you through strong statements, who provokes you with challenging words, who demands that you notice who you're talking to, is signaling the need for appreciation.

Appreciation-based communication looks like:
Expect to see big gestures. He is the kind of person that will take up more space and gladly move into yours. His facial expressions may seem exaggerated, with eyebrows up and a big open-mouthed smile.

Appreciation-based communication reads in e-mail:
In messages, he will offer a story or humorous anecdote to illustrate a point. Occasionally, he may send you jokes, funny pictures, and links to humorous clips to show that he's thinking of you and that he wants your appreciation for it.

The Appreciation Click

Be direct and enthusiastic! Recognize and acknowledge the person you are talking to. Use your words and attitude to create a spotlight effect. Let her know she is important, and important to you, by the way you talk. Let the sound of your voice be energized by the chance to talk with her. Find opportunities for acknowledgment and appreciation for what she says. Ask for input. Ask for advice. Ask for her help. Ask for her insight. Ask for her experiences. All of these invitations tell the person "I value you."

Helpful Phrases for the Appreciation Click:

"I noticed how **you** . . ."

"I love the way **you** . . ."

"How do **you** . . ."

"Can **you** show me . . ."

"What do **you** think?"

"Help me with something."

Mixing and Matching Styles

Most communication problems come down to mismatched styles. If the person you are interacting with is focused on the goal side of things, and you follow your usual m.o. by being more intent on the people side of things, you may be considered a distraction and you won't make the connection. The worst way to get someone using an accuracy style to hurry up is to demand action; the best way to bring him along is by meeting him where he is, and then going forward a step or two at a time. If a person likes to go into detail, while you get right to the heart of the matter, you're going to have to consciously moderate yourself when you want to connect.

Most communication problems come down
to mismatched styles.

When you meet someone whose communication style matches your own, clicking can proceed smoothly. Matching styles, though, isn't always the best way to connect. If you and the other person both use action-based communication, for example, one of you may be eclipsed by the other person. If you both are driving toward your own vision of a result, you are headed for a crash. Instead, you need to acknowledge her desire for action, recognize her vision, then come out with your alternative. Present your alternative as a way of getting her to her desired result. You may go a couple of rounds, but ultimately it will earn you her respect.

When two people are both using approval-based communication, it can lead to indecision and procrastination. It's the *Marty* dilemma: "What do you want to do?" "I don't know, what do *you* want to do?" But by providing some direction you can move things along and, at the same time, click.

It's a good idea to have a clue about where you are starting from in any given situation. What's your style? What is most important to you in communication? How can you shift the emphasis of your behavior to match the other person's style while not abandoning your own? Identifying your own preferred styles will illuminate what makes it harder for you to click with some people than with others.

Things Change

Communication is a pattern of behavior, not a type of personality, and as such, it is subject to change. The more familiar people are with one another, the more likely that other behaviors will emerge. Someone's style can change depending on the situation, whether it's public or private, whether it's just a few people or many people, whether there are financial pressures, and whether it's driven by fear or desire. It can change based on priorities in a moment in time.

So you can never assume you've figured someone out once and for all. Keep pitching to what you know she's hitting, but be ready with a change-up when it's called for. To do that, you have to keep paying attention, so you'll know when things change. You might be able to get along just fine with the other guy on your project team when it's just you and him. But when your boss is in the room, suddenly his straight-ahead action style gives way to approval. If you want to keep working together smoothly, you're going to have to adjust your style, too.

Your own flexibility is the key to building relationships with others.

Practice, Practice, Practice

The best way to learn how to recognize all four communication styles is to practice using them.

- Identify a specific person with whom you want to click, and the specific situation in which you want to click. Then ask yourself: What will your attention focus on? What is a goal that you have? Or, what other people are involved in the situation?

- If you have a goal in mind, are you more concerned with the process or the outcome? Is the other person more concerned with the process or the outcome?
- When you speak, are you faster or slower, more direct or indirect? What is the other person's speech like?
- Are you more concerned with how the other person feels or how you are perceived by him? How about the other person?

Another useful exercise is to try saying the same thing using each style. Start where you are. If you know the details, what's the point? If you know the point, what are the steps to the process? If you know how you feel, start by trying to understand the feelings of others. If you know how others feel, try saying how you feel instead.

Saying It Four Ways

"Building connection with people has many benefits."

- Action: "Build connections, get benefits."

- Accuracy: "Experts have found that building connection with people is a valid way of increasing the size of one's network. It is a worthwhile way to go about building a safety net, and therefore this is an idea worthy of consideration."

- Approval: "What do you think about building connections with people? Do you think that would have any benefits for you? I've heard it's a good thing to do. Don't you agree?"

- Appreciation: "If I were you, I'd get busy building connections with people. It's great for you, great for them, everyone wins. Trust me on this. You do what I say, someday you'll thank me because they'll be thanking you."

When you can say anything four different ways, you can get along with just about anyone in any situation.

CHAPTER 5

Motivation to Click

CONNECTING AND CLICKING IS NOT ABOUT MOTIVATING someone, it's about figuring out what his motivation is, and how to satisfy it.

You can't really motivate anyone else. People don't ever do what you want them to do simply because you want them to do it. They do what they do because *they* want to do it. Because they have a reason—they have a *motivation* to do it. Or a motivation not to do it. Or no motivation, so they do nothing. There's a motive behind every decision, every behavior. Motivation determines determination and drives drive. When you learn to identify someone's motivation and tap into it, you can create all this and more.

If you understand the motivational drivers of human behavior, then you can gain the ability to identify and engage these drivers in yourself and in your relationships. Understand what motivates you and you can express yourself with more clarity and focus. Understand someone else's motivation and you'll know what to say and how to say it, whenever you want to click. Then you'll be ready to send signals of motivational similarity, speak to a person as an insider rather than an outsider, reach people at a deeper level of who they are, and make a powerful connection. Click!

It all starts by wondering why.

Motivation: Moving Toward, Moving Away

Motivation is all about movement. At our most basic level of existence, we are motivated by our desires and our fears. While we have all kinds of motivations, we will always move toward desire or away from fear. Either we want something enough to do something about it, or we don't want something enough to prevent it.

The signs for both motivations are telltale. Those motivated by fear move away from a threat, while those motivated by desire will do what they can to get what they want. The good news is that you can work with both types of motivation to achieve your desire—the click.

Matching Motivation

Let's say you have an idea for a project to make your office more efficient. Lately, the mail system has fallen to pieces, and no one is sure who is delivering the mail, who receives it in which department, and when the mail cart comes around to pick it up. After weeks of missing bills and lost issues of your newsletter, you've figured out a foolproof plan to get everyone their mail quickly and efficiently. While you're excited about this new plan, the project's successful implementation involves the participation of your coworkers, some of whom you hardly know. When you present your project idea to them, their response is flat and disengaged. What's missing isn't your motivation. It's theirs.

> Motivation comes down to how a person answers these fundamental questions: "What's in it for me?" and "Why should I care?"

If your coworkers don't share your motivation for your project, you have to help them find it. Motivation comes down to how a person answers these fundamental questions: "What's in it for me?" and "Why should I care?" If you want your project to move forward, you will have to help your coworkers ask these questions and find good answers.

Claudia faced a dilemma much like this. After having worked for her software company for some time, she had an idea for a new product line. Before presenting it, she developed a project overview and a proposal. It looked great on paper, and her boss told her to build a team to execute it. Her first pick for her team was Jan, who had strong connections with industry insiders who might be of great value in pulling certain parts of the project together.

When Claudia introduced the idea, however, Jan's response was lukewarm. She reluctantly agreed to a small role on the team, but made it clear she didn't think much of the idea. The more excited Claudia was about the project, the more Jan seemed to pull back. As time passed, Claudia found herself defending her idea with Jan instead of advancing it, and feeling more and more frustrated, disappointed, and angry.

Claudia realized she needed to understand Jan's motivation if she was to have any chance of getting Jan's help. She listened to how Jan talked about other issues and ideas in the office, and learned that Jan, regardless of the topic, spoke a lot about what she didn't want, and only rarely about what she did want. Claudia also heard Jan telling another employee, "That's not what I do," and "That's really not my job." Hope was not lost, though, because she'd overheard Jan arguing passionately when someone trespassed on the turf of her expertise. She'd declare, "I do this because I'm good at it, so stay out of my way and let me do my job!"

Here was someone with great connections and skills who doubted her own abilities when she was outside her comfort zone. Jan resisted new opportunity out of fear of failure. As a result, she stayed with the familiar. Jan was moving away from Claudia's project out of fear of failure. Claudia decided to help Jan get what she wanted—to stay in her domain of competence and success—and avoid what spooked her—being exposed to criticism and judgment if the project failed. Claudia needed to limit the possibility of failure falling on Jan and assure her she could stay in familiar territory. After all, it was the software designers, not the team leader, who would be boldly going where they'd never gone before. Claudia also needed to show Jan the downside of not coming onboard, in order to speak to her "away" motivation.

Claudia approached, having rehearsed in her mind what she would say. "Jan, this project I'm asking you to get involved with . . . there's something I don't think I made clear to you. It's my project and if it doesn't work out, it's on me, and our manager knows that. I won't ask you to do anything that you haven't done on other projects. If you have a problem with anything I ask of you, tell me your specific concern and I'll find a way to deal with it. You're perfect for this, and you know the right people who could make this project a success. It would be a real shame if you failed to notice that. I'm only asking you to do what only you know how to do. If you don't contribute your expertise to this project, I really think you'll be missing out."

Click!

Jan agreed to come on board as long as her exposure was limited, and on the condition that she wouldn't have to do anything she wasn't competent at doing. It wasn't that Jan didn't have motivation. It was that Claudia hadn't engaged her motivation.

Sometimes building a connection means finding out what someone really wants in a way that she knows you get it, or will help her get it. And sometimes it means finding out what someone doesn't want, and then helping her avoid it. Sometimes it's a little of both.

Fear as a Motivator

Fear commands interest and holds it, at least initially. The oldest and most despised trick in the persuasion book is to get a person to feel threatened and then offer an easy solution that eliminates the threat. It's practically guaranteed, in the short term, to generate interest and engage motivation. But those who use it this way should be warned: They must walk a fine line when using fear to motivate. Apply too little and it won't gain any interest. Apply too much and they overload and exhaust the receptors for it, with the paradoxical effect of loss of interest.

Fear has a place in our lives as a powerful motivational force. It protected our ancestors from saber-toothed tigers, and today it may get you across a busy street safely. And it can hold your feet to the fire of a promise made when the rest of you wants to fly away from that promise. You will find it useful to add a little fear anytime you are motivated by desire. Desire will move you forward when you have energy to spare, and fear will keep you going when your energy flags. That's the best way to use fear . . . as a seasoning for your commitments. Take into account what you stand to lose by not taking action, and it may get your feet moving in the desirable direction.

For example, you would think that a person would learn the lesson provided by a speeding ticket: Don't speed. And sure enough, in the two weeks following a speeding ticket, a driver will typically behave better on the road. But it doesn't take long for the fear motivation to wear off, and the old behavior to kick in. Soon, that driver is back up to his old tricks. Or he's learned a new one, such as: You can avoid tickets if you just pay closer attention to overpasses and on-ramps. When the fear wears off, the driver is left with whatever motivated the speeding in the first place.

> Desire will move you forward when you have energy to spare, and fear will keep you going when your energy flags.

While fear plays an important role in motivation, it cannot create sustained motivation by itself. Even when the people you want to click with are using it on themselves, it's in your interest to keep the short-term nature of fear motivation in mind, and to find a greater desire to keep motivation alive. To click with people motivated by fear, you need to speak to their fear.

The rule for using fear as a motivator in our own lives is that a little bit goes a long way.

Desire as a Motivator

Desire is a strong and sustainable force. It can light a fire in your belly, or get you to take a chance—or even risk failure. If you know why something matters to you, you can go further, deeper, or higher than you've ever gone before.

You begin to identify desire when you can answer the question, "What do you want?" Someone who is motivated by fear will answer, "I *don't want* to feel bad." Use this as your chance to move things forward. Acknowledge the fear and ask, "Then what *do* you want to feel?"

The answer is something you can connect over, something worthwhile—perhaps something you can work toward together.

Sometimes it takes people a little while to arrive at a useful answer to this powerful question. They might reply with a comparative statement like "I want to feel better than this." Keep talking to them until you can get a positive answer; desire is about what you want to work toward.

Name it and claim it.

The 6 Types of Motivation

Motivation drives behavior and determines what someone is paying attention to and how he will interpret any attention you give him. Our interest here is to consider the motivations more subtle than survival that are at play in modern humans. There is a full spectrum of concerns another person may be working with that you need to tap into if you want to click.

I'm going to break motivation down into six recognizable categories that can help you to understand yourself and others, motivations with which you can click. Each type has an aspect of both fear and desire.

Values
Reward
Challenge
Esteem

Purpose

Feelings

Just as people's lives are complex, our motivations are many. We don't have one motivation for everything we do. What motivates us depends on where we are, who we are with, and what is before us or behind us.

If you can understand a person's primary motivation, the one that is more important than the others in a given situation, you can frame what you say in a way that speaks to that primary motivation, which will lead to a more meaningful click.

1. Values

It is next to impossible to convince a person primarily motivated by her values to go along with something she perceives as "wrong," and almost impossible to stop such a person from doing something she believes to be right.

To put it into perspective, say one evening while you're driving home late on the highway, you notice someone who appears to be injured and attempting to hitchhike. You know it is wrong to pick up hitchhikers, especially so late at night. Equally, you've been instilled with a sense of stewardship and you can tell this person needs help. What do you do? It's a serious question. Should you pass him by, you may agonize over it long past the point where it is still relevant to making a choice. If you pick him up, it could be dangerous.

Values are a significant element in how cultures and societies are structured. Conflict over values is often found at the heart of the most divisive issues we face in our society. So values are potential tripwires in any relationship. One of the first things you should ferret out about a person at the outset of any relationship is his system of values. It's a good idea to check out the shared values underlying any new group you join, too.

When people are motivated by their sense of right and wrong, they tend to divide the world into black-and-white terms. The person who desires to do the right thing squares his shoulders, sucks in his gut, and steps boldly forward. The person in fear of doing something wrong may struggle for air during his internal debate, then shrug his shoulders to dismiss the question or opportunity.

> Ethics isn't always a choice between right and wrong. Sometimes it's choosing between two rights and sometimes it's choosing the lesser of two evils.

The world is *not* all black and white. Most issues involving value judgments of right and wrong fall in that big gray area between the rule of law and free will known as ethics. Ethics isn't always a choice between right and wrong. Sometimes it's choosing between two rights, and sometimes it's choosing the lesser of two evils.

Clicking with Someone Motivated by Values

You can hear when a person's sense of right and wrong is her primary motivation; her speech will be riddled with words like *should* and *must*, or *shall not* and *should not*. People motivated by values tend to speak with great conviction, as if something important depends on what they advocate being just, reasonable, and fair.

Phrases Associated with Values:

- *"It isn't right,"* and *"It's only fair."*
- *"We are obligated to do this."*
- *"It's only right that I talk with you."*
- *"It seems proper to discuss this first."*

If a person speaks often about doing the right thing, you can frame your interactions with her accordingly. Bring up a situation where you chose to do the right thing, even if it wasn't the most popular decision. When making a suggestion or responding to something she's said, use similar buzzwords. Sentences like, *"You really should consider this,"* or *"It seems only fair that you hear me out,"* will really resonate with that individual. With the person who appears to be motivated by a strong sense of prudence and a desire to avoid the morally repugnant, you'll hear her commenting on what would be wrong or improper. Frame your conversations with her accordingly.

Talk about avoiding mistakes, about preventing injustice, about the unfairness of not considering something or taking a certain action. When speaking with her, speak to this sense of prudence with sentences such as, *"It would be a terrible injustice if we didn't meet,"* and *"It seems we should discuss the matter."*

2. Reward

Some people are moved to action when there is something they stand to gain or something they stand to lose. Winning and losing are powerful enough motivators that entire industries have been set up to serve them. It doesn't take big gains and losses to move people. Incentive programs, for example, leverage the desire to gain. Prize contests, sales, and bonuses all operate through the motivation of reward. Sometimes a kind word or a smile can be reward enough, just as the disapproval of a coach or mentor can be a loss to be avoided.

Motivation that's driven by the hunger for reward is often brought into play with the promise of a gift or the idea of something good yet to come. Watch and observe, listen and attend, because when a person is moved by the promise of reward, she'll tell you. You can see it in her excited nod as she gazes ahead. You can hear it in the enthusiasm in her voice when she speaks about the object of her desire. Often these individuals enjoy taking risks or trying new things.

A person driven by the fear of loss will back away from that possibility in word and deed, shaking his head at the mere prospect of it. "I don't think I'm willing to take that chance" or "Too rich for my blood." This motivation leads some to set impossible conditions before agreeing to pursue a reward, hoping that the inability for those conditions to be met will guarantee that there will be no loss.

I know a guy who wanted to get into real estate investing. (This was back before the bubble burst.) But it scared the heck out of him. So every time he made an offer on a property, he made it lower than the recommendation of his Realtor, hoping to be outbid and thus protected from making a mistake and losing everything. Turns out that when the market turned south and so many people lost so much in real estate, he gained the reward of knowing that his fearful approach had been a good one. That reward for his caution will likely motivate more caution in other matters for years to come.

Clicking with Someone Motivated by Reward

Individuals driven by a desire for rewards will use some of the same language that surrounds mathematics. Things *"add up,"* or they are *"on the money."* You'll hear someone talk about how he can *"add a little here and subtract a little something over there,"* and *"stack the deck in my favor."* If you hear the language of reward, speak to it.

If a person speaks often about *winning*, *obtaining*, or *getting more*, you can frame your interactions with her accordingly. Talk about how rewarding it is to meet her, how working or being together is a real *"win,"* and how taking action now will ensure you *"both come out ahead."*

Some phrases to consider:

- *"This conversation will benefit us both."*
- *"We stand to gain a lot from this."*

If a person demonstrates this motivational pattern by frequently talking about *losing* or *missing out, being deprived,* or *not receiving her due,* respond in kind. You can frame your conversations around including her and pointing out the potential for gain.

Try using phrases such as:

- *"Because I don't want you to miss out, we should get while the getting is good."*
- *"I didn't want to lose this chance to meet you."*

When offering a reward, be careful that you're giving it for good behavior. A reward for doing nothing, for example, reinforces doing nothing. If you reward negative behavior with a lot of attention, you'll be sure to see it again. Rewarding complaints with reaction may get you more complaints, but preventing complaints by rewarding pro-action may eliminate the need for complaints at all.

Some rewards are external, like the little sound of pleasure a person makes when you give him a gift or do something that he enjoys. Other rewards are intrinsic, which can be more motivating and more powerful in the end. These are the kinds of rewards we feel within, such as a sense of accomplishment or pride after finishing a project.

3. Challenge (Success/Failure)

The challenge motivation is about the thrill of trying and is the driving force behind athletic prowess, academic achievement, business building, and artistic endeavor. Challenge-seekers are risk takers, and often don't give up easily. They will keep trying until they feel that thrill of victory or that agony of defeat.

Some people will eagerly take up a challenge as a group that they wouldn't touch on their own, counting on the motivation of others to pick up the slack if necessary. And the reverse is also true. Some people would never dream of taking up a challenge if it meant placing their fate in the hands of others.

"Because it is there." That's what British climber George Mallory said, when asked why he wanted to climb Mount Everest. He disappeared, along with his climbing partner Andrew Irvine, before he ever reached the summit. He had to know that he risked being defeated by the harsh conditions before he ever began. But so strong was his motivation that all he could see was the chance for a victorious climb. That is exactly the way a person motivated by challenge sees what is before her. "It is there, therefore I must."

People positively motivated by challenge display the qualities of champions, of those who successfully tread the path to ultimate victory: passion, vision, preparation, goal-setting, planning, mental and physical training, perseverance, courage, and integrity.

Clicking with Someone Motivated by Challenge

The language of challenge is about success and failure, victory and defeat, overcoming or succumbing, and rising or falling. If someone wants to be successful, and you have something to contribute to his success, he will want to hear you out about it. Likewise, if he is more focused on avoiding being part of a losing team, you should offer him a safe alternative should things go wrong.

Frame your interactions in the language of success, just as he does. Talk about how you share his can-do spirit, how working or being together will lead to success, and how taking action now will ensure victory.

Some phrases to keep in mind:

- *"This is our chance to meet this challenge head on."*
- *"We will be triumphant."*
- *"Here's what we can do."*

You should also respond in kind to the person who demonstrates this motivational pattern by talking about defeat, failure, and what can't be done.

Try these phrases on for size:

- *"We can't let this moment pass us by."*
- *"We will not be defeated."*
- *"You can only fail if you do not try."*
- *"If I failed to introduce myself to you, I'd never forgive myself for letting the opportunity slip away."*

Click!

4. Esteem

Esteem motivates the drive for reputation and fame. People driven by this motivation seek to make their mark on the world in order to increase their sense of worthiness. It's easy to notice people driven by the esteem motivation because they engage in obvious behavior designed to draw attention to themselves and increase their standing in the eyes of others.

Mary Kay Ash, founder of Mary Kay Cosmetics, famously said that people want only two things more than sex and money: recognition and praise. She was no doubt describing her own motivation, while recognizing the powerful role it plays in the lives of others. To the person motivated by esteem, recognition is like oxygen.

People with this motivation may assume it exists in everyone else. They give recognition and appreciation eagerly, believing that it will reflect favorably on them. It's a good strategy, too, because people appreciate those who appreciate them, and give recognition to people who deem them worthy of recognition. But not all who are driven by this motivation are as generous in the recognition they give. Some are hard on themselves, and just as hard on everyone else. "You can always do better," and "Nobody's perfect," are verbal indicators of people who may struggle with their own self-worth.

When esteem is the motivation, there is no greater insult than someone getting a name wrong, or not remembering someone at all. It's not uncommon for the person with this motivation to declare loudly, "Don't you know who I am?"

This actually happened when I was at the airport in Chicago. Our flight was cancelled, and the rebooking line at the counter was long. Someone motivated by his own sense of importance pushed his way to the head of the line and demanded attention from the woman behind the counter. She asked him to wait his turn.

He practically bellowed, "Don't you know who I am?"

She took this as a cue to pick up the microphone and make the following announcement. "There is a gentleman at the counter who doesn't know who he is. If you do, would you please come and claim him?"

Embarrassed and ashamed, he slunk away.

The agent may not have gotten a click with him (though she certainly did with the others waiting in line), but she did tap into his motivation accurately, triggering the fear response.

When people with this motivation don't feel respected, they may treat others with disrespect. They tend to be defensive, arguing with anyone who seems to contradict them, and strive mightily to avoid being singled out for criticism or disdain, or a bad reputation. If they are dominated by low self-esteem, they may keep their head down and their mouth shut, only offering their ideas when prodded repeatedly. The fear often leads to mistakes and shame, embarrassment and self-doubt. You can hear them disrespecting themselves in the way they dismiss what they say as soon as they say it: "You probably already thought of that," and "It's not really important."

Clicking with Someone Motivated by Esteem

Listen for admonishments to be proud, to be independent, to stand up for yourself, or to develop your unique gifts and abilities and be all that you can be. Find a way to let people with this motivation be somebody, in your eyes, or in the eyes of others. Put them in charge of something (even something small) and then give them recognition for taking it on. Ask for them to share their wisdom with you. All of these approaches send the signal: "You are someone special and worthwhile, and I recognize you for it."

5. Feelings

When all is said and done, pleasure and pain are really the only two motivational forces in life. We find pleasure in doing what's right, in gaining a reward, in taking on a challenge, in developing our worth, in living with purpose. It is the avoidance of pain that drives us away from doing what's wrong, from losing, from failing and, from feeling worthless and empty.

Pain can motivate people to do terrible things, from lashing out in self-defense to violence and other aggression aimed at stopping the pain altogether. Likewise, the promise of pleasure has motivated people to do all kinds of things that may or may not have been in their interest, including binge eating, drug addiction, and marital infidelity. We know that some people are drawn toward pleasure like moths toward a flame. They know something is wrong, and yet they must do it anyway. And some people find pleasure in pain, either in their own pain or in the pain of others.

Clicking with Someone Motivated by Feelings

If you aren't able to identify someone's motivation, or her motivation doesn't fit well into the other categories in this model of motivation, to click you should speak to the desire for pleasure and the fear of pain. You do this by talking about feelings.

Below are some sentences to use in such a situation:

- *"It's a pleasure to meet you."*
- *"Won't it feel good to get together?"*
- *"I'm sure there is something we can do to ease the pain and frustration you've been going through."*

6. Purpose

Purpose is one of the strongest motivational forces of all, because it gives us fulfillment. Without purpose, action seems empty, and emptiness is often the harbinger of darkness and despair. A person motivated by a sense of purpose ultimately does what she does because it fulfills her at the core of who she is. She knows who she is, why she is, and why she must keep going. Just the desire for a sense of purpose in life is itself a motivator for action. Purpose exists beyond material benefit, beyond reward. Purpose is what gives life real meaning. Purpose is the biggest reason why.

There comes a time in our lives when living with purpose outweighs all other considerations, and finding our purpose promises the way out of that sense of emptiness when we have no idea what we are supposed to be doing. A life driven by purpose expresses itself in the language of idealism, of a perfect world, of how things ought to be, of the meaning of life: *"This is what I'm meant to be doing,"* "In a perfect world . . . ," "Here's how I fit in . . ." The purposeless person expresses futility and hopelessness because when he looks to the past, he sees no point, and when he looks to the future, he finds nothing there compelling enough to pursue: "I don't see the point," "Why bother?," "Like *that*'s going to do any good . . ."

Clicking with Someone Motivated by Purpose

Understand the power of purpose and convey your understanding. Notice when someone talks about the meaning of his life, and support that same purpose in the way you respond. Connect to his sense of purpose or some aspect of it. Or help someone along the path to finding his purpose by talking about his idea of the ideal, and the values he brings to making that happen. Because purpose is such a broad motivation, conversation can be wide-ranging and still connect. The key is to speak in terms of how things ought to be, why we are here, and asking about what his biggest dreams and ambitions are for making the world a better place. Talk about what the action is, why that's what's happening, and why it matters. To tap into a sense of purpose, start with phrases like, "This is why we are here," "Here's why what we're doing makes a difference," "Everything has brought us to this moment," or "This is where it all begins to count." The most effective way to connect to purpose is to be specific about the purpose: "This is about producing a quality product," say, or "We're all about saving the rain forest."

How to Identify Motivation

Sometimes motivation is obvious, a matter of bringing to the forefront what has been in the background all along. Much of the time, people will simply tell you what their motivations are. If you listen to how people explain, defend, justify, and excuse themselves—you'll hear such things in the regular course of any conversation—you can learn a lot about their motivations. Listen to the reasons why people say they do what they do, and don't do what they don't do. Just listen.

Motivational Layering

People layer or stack their motivations, starting with their most important driver, but this layering is not progressive, it's additive. The more motivations someone has, the more motivated she will be.

The most basic version of motivational layering takes place when you mix a little fear with a lot of desire—the mix that's proven to be the most effective. The person who has something to move toward and something to leave behind has more motivation to keep trying than the person with only one or the other.

Not all fears carry the same weight, nor does every desire. Some fears and desires speak more powerfully to some individuals than others do. Discerning the layers and addressing them in turn makes for the most powerful connections.

Use *why* to identify a person's motivations and to understand the way those motivations are layered. If you ask "Why do you want to go to that conference?" and someone tells you "Everyone's going," you can keep asking, gently not intrusively, and you'll soon know the range and depth of everything that is influencing their behavior—including how many forms of motivation. You'll have a deeper connection with people by letting them tell you their reasons why, and understanding them.

Some potential responses include:

Esteem

"It's a chance for me to be noticed by my professional peers."

"If I don't show up, my associates might assume I don't care about developing my skills."

Values

> *"They're counting on me."*
>
> *"I wouldn't want to let them down."*

Challenge

> *"It's a real chance to learn from the top experts in the field!"*
>
> *"I'd hate to miss something that would let others pass me by."*

Feelings

> *"It would be fun!"*
>
> *"I'd hate to miss all the fun."*

If You Want to Know Someone's Motivation, Ask for It

Sometimes the best thing to do is to set everything aside and just ask, "Why are you doing that?" You don't want to ask these questions so bluntly with most people. But finding out the answers connects you to people in incredibly deep and meaningful ways. You can soften the questions by asking for their help.

- *"Can you help me understand why you do this?"*
- *"I'd really like to know you better. Can you tell me why you care so much about that?"*

Once you've reached a certain level of connection—once you know the *who, what, where, when,* and *how* of something said to you—asking why gives you a deeper level of understanding and insight into what makes someone tick, and tells you exactly how to click.

That's what I did the day my wife came into my office, sat on my couch, and told me that she'd just spoken with a friend on the phone. When I asked who it was, my wife declined to tell me. I knew that she had a reason to refrain from telling me, but the fact that she told me anything at all told me she wanted to share at least something.

I was curious so I asked. "Honey, you brought this up, told me just enough to get me interested, and then stopped. I'm curious, why won't you tell me the rest of it?"

Looking away, she said, "It would be wrong."

I continued to push. "Why would it be wrong?"

Hesitantly, she finally conceded, "I can't tell you because I want you to know you can trust me not to violate your confidence."

In this, I could hear that she was motivated by what she didn't want. She was concerned about doing the wrong thing, and behind all of that was her wanting my respect. Her concerns and motivations were both based on fear, values, and esteem.

I had the idea to use the moment to reinforce something that motivates me: the fact that it is important to me, as a doctor, that my private conversations with my wife be kept in confidence.

So I told my wife that I would never want her ever to do something she thought was wrong, and I had nothing but the greatest respect for the way she honored our private conversations. In that moment, I may not have gotten what I initially wanted (details on my wife's conversation with her friend) but I got something far more valuable to me: an even deeper connection with my wife.

There's nothing particularly remarkable about that conversation. But by choosing to listen for motivation, I could hear what was there all along. And asking about it produced a click.

You Go First

The fastest way to learn how to hear and understand motivation in others is to understand your own first. When you get you, others are going to get you too. Whenever something matters to you, get to the bottom of it and find out what makes you tick. Whenever you don't care about something, or are avoiding something, or even denying something, you have a golden opportunity to explore your "away" motivations. As you become familiar with the language you use in exploring these motivations in yourself, you will find it all the more easy to recognize that same language, and resonate with it, when you hear it being used by others.

The most valuable part of this challenge is that it increases your ability to connect with people and provides you with the most pleasurable relationships. It doesn't matter that you get it just right. What matters is that you hear more, and thus know more, and are better able to connect as a result. Because in the moment that you connect with people, they connect with you.

CHAPTER 6

What My Cowbell Says About Me: Identifying Values to Click

WHEN YOU STEP INTO MY OFFICE, YOU WILL SEE MY VALUES written, literally, on the walls. There's my "Be Alive" poster, and my "God Bless America" Peter Max print. There's the "All I need to know about life I learned from *Star Trek*" framed poster over my desk, near the CAPTAIN'S QUARTERS sign. You can see I value something about travel and adventure because my souvenirs are on display, like the wooden flowers from Bali, the cowbell from Switzerland, and the poison dart blowgun from Java. You can see who my heroes are, because there are framed images and reminders on my walls (Buckminster Fuller, Thomas Jefferson, John Lennon, Superman). I daresay you can tell I value a full and varied life, because there is nothing spartan about my office.

Our Values Are on Display Wherever We Are

What a person values is no great mystery. People tell you all the time. This information is in the choices we make, the things we do, the items that surround us in our personal space, and, of course, in the things we say to each other. You can tell when people value health, because they exercise and they eat right. You can tell when people value fun, because they demonstrate it by going to parties and taking trips for pleasure. You can tell when people value hard work, love of country, love of God, or philosophy.

Values guide people in setting goals, making decisions, relating to friends and colleagues, developing plans, and taking actions—and pretty much anything else they undertake. Knowing what others value, and learning how to establish shared values, puts you in a great position to click. When you notice what's important to people, you'll be able to meet people in the areas that mean the most to them. Knowing what others value tells us how they measure everything—their time, their energy, their thoughts—and gives us a point of contact with deep roots. When you can identify values you already share with a person, and find values to share, you'll create a great platform on which to make a connection and build a relationship. Just be sure you do it honestly, or any platform you do manage to make will be shaky at best, and uncomfortable for sure.

Madeline was able to harness one of her coworker's values to turn an unpleasant work relationship into a positive one. She had been working with a guy named Frank for months now. She and Frank seemed to be from different worlds, and whenever they were near each other, those worlds collided. Madeline was easygoing and open, often bringing in baked goods for her colleagues and curious to see photos of everyone's children. Frank, on the other hand, was dour and closed. The shades in his office were always down and when he greeted anyone in the hallway, on the rare occasions he bothered to, he simply grunted. Her voice was high and lilting. His was a deep gravelly rumble. Despite these dramatic differences, Madeline was determined to find a way to click with the man she had to interact with every single working day.

After a while, it wasn't just that Madeline liked to get along with everybody, it was that she felt that her cold relationship with Frank was getting in the way of her work. It bothered her that after all the time they'd worked together, he still couldn't be at least a little friendly to her. One day, Madeline forced herself to march into Frank's office, where she planned to confront him about his cold and unfriendly manner. She walked in, he looked up, and as their eyes made contact, she had second thoughts. His eyebrows were looking especially harsh that day and she wasn't sure if she could stand up to him. Maybe this was a bad idea. She looked around, trying to think of a way out. That's when she saw it. On Frank's desk there was a framed and polished picture of a classic red-and white-convertible automobile which she had never taken note of before.

"Is that your car, Frank?" she asked, then held her breath. This *is* a bad idea, she thought to herself as the silence stretched between them.

But then Frank broke the silence. "Yes it is!" he said. It was the same deep, rumbling voice Madeline had heard for years.

Only this time, there was energy in it. This was something he cared about, thought important, wanted to share. "It's my 1956 T-Bird. I love that car. It's got these amazing rounded tail fins, dual exhaust exits at the side corners of the bumpers, and portholes in the removable hard top. It belonged to my mother . . ."

He couldn't stop talking! His voice, his face, all those elements she'd been taking personally disappeared. His story revealed his love for his mother, his appreciation for all things classic, his attention to detail, and the freedom he experienced when driving on the open road. Madeline had made contact simply by pointing to something Frank valued and asking about it. As it turned out, she valued some of the same things (mothers, freedom, attention to detail . . .), and this gave them something to move forward with.

Click.

If not the beginning of a beautiful friendship, it was at last the start of a real relationship.

Like Attracted to Like

Organizations can rally their people around a clearly defined set of values. Once the people understand and accept those values as the best way to fulfill their own values, they will willingly conduct themselves in a way that does just that. Decisions can be made based on what matters most when there is a high degree of certainty about what is considered right and what is considered wrong, because people click with the values driving the decisions.

Les Schwab Tires is considered by many to be a fringe benefit of living in the Pacific Northwest. They are known for practically legendary customer service, and have tremendous customer loyalty because of it. Every employee exemplifies the mission statement: "Pride in Performance is the value that drives us at Les Schwab. We take pride in our customer service and pride in our employees. As a company we try to incorporate this belief into everything we do." Employees click with these values, and customers click with the employees.

Patagonia, the outdoor clothing company, values a pristine environment. When they state what they value, they qualify it like this: "Our reason for being is to make the best product and cause no unnecessary harm. Yet we are keenly aware that everything we do as a business—or have done in our name—leaves its mark on the environment. As yet, there is no such thing as a sustainable business, but every day we take steps to lighten our footprint and do less harm."

> When people come together around these values, they get each other, and are able to bring out the best in each other.

People are driven by their own values to work for a company like this. And when people come together around these values, they get each other, and are able to bring out the best in each other. They click.

The reverse is also true. When teams and partners can't agree on what matters most, the differences will tear them apart. Organizations with no clear set of values lack a coherent center around which leaders can lead and people can organize. The result is turf wars, backbiting, and disciplinary issues. People who have nothing but the platitude of values, like "I believe in family values," or "It is wrong to do wrong," are left with no recourse but to poke and point at values they don't recognize as their own. When all you know is what you don't want, it undermines your credibility and costs you the support of others. Competing values are often at the foundation of conflict. Values are so central to our lives that they have become a convenient wedge for divide-and-conquer strategies in the political realm, in the media, in the workplace, and in communities.

> When all you know is what you don't want, it undermines your credibility and costs you the support of others.

People get intensely excited, upset, and even irrational when something they value seems threatened. Ironically, even people who aren't quite sure what their values are become strong defenders of them, most likely because they recognize that there is something basic, essential, and compelling about what matters most in life. For example, family values is a broad label that can mean different things to different people. People can be adamant about family values yet be unable to tell you which family values (love, respect, diversity, faithfulness, hierarchy, duty, unity) they adhere to. Protesters march in the street because they are anti-war, or against a trade agreement. Yet if you ask what the values are that moved them into the street, all they can do *is* mouth the slogans written on their signs. Their passions are engaged around something, but they are not quite sure what it is. All they know is that something about it clicked for them, and they are willing to march for it.

Using Values to Click

Simply professing certain values doesn't guarantee success or fulfillment. You have to act on your values to fulfill them. Begin by making an honest appraisal of how someone (or some organization) *is acting* on her values. Look around at her environment, listen to what people say about her, consider her track record. Take an inventory of her behavior and use that as a barometer of what matters most, and then work your way back to what values that embodies. Say your boss always seems to be in meetings. She always has time for one, can't get enough of the office confab. Think, why all the meetings? Based on your experience in your workplace, you may realize most of those meetings are about communication and strategy—common workplace values. Now, even as someone who hates sitting around conference room tables for any reason, you have grounds for clicking: Valuing communication and strategy is something you can get behind. *Click.*

> You have to act on your values to fulfill them.

Local politics recently gave me a chance to see this kind of click at work in real life. As head of the school board, Harriet was eager for Jacob to run for a third term. Jacob had been a valued member of the board through his two terms. He'd really helped turn the organization around, transforming the disorganized, in-fighting, closed-off board that he'd joined into an efficient, cooperative, and open group. As a result, they were making better decisions, receiving more public support, and able to do more good work for the community they served. But now Jacob was ready for a new challenge. He felt satisfied the board would be able to continue on its positive path without him.

Harriet disagreed. Jacob's energy, passion, and enthusiasm had been crucial in bringing about numerous positive changes on the board, in the schools, and in the community. She wanted Jacob to run for a third term, but how could she accomplish that? Having worked with him for both his terms, Harriet had heard plenty about Jacob's values. She knew he valued efficiency, because she'd heard him comment in their board meetings that "Inefficient systems are shamefully wasteful," and "We need to make better use out of the resources available to us." She knew from watching him and talking with him that he found pleasure in designing and tweaking systems, and had heard him speak of the importance of a design matching its intent. She knew he valued his own learning process, because he had told her years ago that he joined the board in order to learn how boards go about their work. And she knew that he valued making a difference because, on more than one occasion, he had simply told her so. Above all, she knew, he valued the conditions that create big opportunities. At several board meetings, he'd used the broken field of football as a metaphor for opportunity. "In football, eleven players per side face off in an orderly manner. The play begins, the players scatter, and where everything was orderly before the play, now chaos covers the field. The gaps," he would say, "are opportunities for big plays." Jacob loved turbulence and turmoil, because they indicated a broken field. Looking at that broken field, Jacob saw not disorder, but possibility.

Harriet suspected that Jacob had lost interest in serving on the school board because the gaps were no longer obvious to him. The board was working well together. The community was more involved, giving more input. They now had systems in place for decision making, for collecting data, for interacting with each other and the surrounding community. It wasn't a broken field. There were no gaps, no opportunities for him to fulfill his values.

It was with this insight into his values that Harriet approached Jacob. Harriet asked if he had yet recognized the biggest problem still facing the school board. Jacob was naturally puzzled, as he believed that he had fulfilled his mandate. Not so, Harriet explained. "There's no recruitment process in place, so the board is only one election away from having all our hard work fall apart. If only we had a way to identify the right people and get them to run for open positions, what a difference that would make for this community." She reminded him of a neighboring community with three open seats that wound up in chaos when they were filled by unqualified people who had run uncontested. "What a shame we never got this handled while we had you." Suddenly, Jacob could see a broken field, an opportunity to make a big difference by designing an efficient system that required him to learn about something new. *Click.*

Obviously, clicking is not always this straightforward. An individual can have competing values. In fact, most people in our culture have been brought up this way, and it causes a great deal of confusion. We are taught to "love thy neighbor as thyself." We are also taught that it's a "dog eat dog world, and you have to look out for number one." How do you make sense out of that? You can't. But you can acknowledge the conflict of it. Oftentimes, these conflicts persist because they remain unconscious and unexamined. If you notice that someone is torn between competing values, you can click with her by bringing this to the surface when you talk with her, exploring the values and their definitions and then talking about what matters most. Prioritizing values helps people resolve these conflicts and think more clearly.

Take Pete, for example. He values his time with his family, yet he also values a good day's hard work. Many are the nights he spends working late, and the side effect is no time with his family. The result is that he feels conflicted most of the time. If you want to click with Pete, talk with him about this conflict. "I know you love your family. It must be difficult for you to be here working so late and missing out on the time with them." Pete will recognize that you are speaking to some important aspect of his life and will click with you because of this. It will likely get him talking, and your ability to listen and draw him out will become a benefit of his knowing you.

Where competing values are at play, you'll see the telltale signs: people or groups sending mixed messages, or unable to make decisions, or consequences of actions upholding one value adversely impacting on another value. Consider the person who values his health but doesn't take the time to exercise because of a competing value such as a priority on down time. Or perhaps thriftiness, which prevents him from shelling out for a gym membership. Notice conflicts like these and engage with people around them, and you create an opportunity to connect with them that is both meaningful and helpful.

The value of recognizing values and values conflicts is that you can talk with people about things that matter to them on a very deep level. And in talking about them, you may even discover something about your own values in the process. You may find there are many values that you share, and that you can share. This is how strong relationships are built. This is how people gain confidence in one another. This is how people help each other to honor the important values in their lives.

Know What You Value

Knowing your own values helps you to notice them in others. And because most people find value in people who are living their values, being able to state yours and act on yours with confidence, clarity, and authority increases your inherent clickability—as well as improves your skill at clicking with someone else.

Begin by asking yourself: What matters most to me in my life? *What do I* think is important enough to find time to bring to fruition?

Most people working up a list like this will find they have between five and ten core values. Only you can say what your values are, but to stimulate your thinking, here are some common values:

Family, honesty, fun, God, learning, adventure, organization, spirit, leadership, laughter, teamwork, integrity, love, creativity, service, joy, children, money, romance, effectiveness, happiness, health, freedom.

Many or even most of those might appeal to you, but you have to identify which are at the top of the heap.

Check your behavior as well as your thoughts. Sure, you might say, I value health highly. But maybe not so much if you're dining at the Golden Arches every day and haven't broken a sweat in ages. Your strongest values are the ones you are most likely to be demonstrably living by.

When Values Conflict

You may disagree with someone on many particulars yet still share values. Focusing on what divides you can prevent a click; working from what unites you can provide one. I walked this line with a potential client who was claiming that Republicans were far superior to Democrats because "We think that limited government is important, but Democrats want government to act as a Big Brother in charge of everything!" A clear values statement, I suppose. But this kind of political pigeonholing violates my own value of transpartisanship and bipartisan relations. I happen to agree with the idea of limits on government, however. So while I was tempted to go three rounds with him about the importance of working together and the problems of declaring oneself to be better than someone else, instead I said, "Yes, I agree, it's important that the size of government be limited." I chose not to break the value down to the details where we might disagree, and paid attention to the value he and I shared. There was no point in doing otherwise.

> When you generalize largely enough, everybody is the same. But if you take in enough details, everyone is different. The goal is to find the common ground. Find values that you can share—not to give your opinion of what should matter most. Build your connection around what matters most to the other person.

Authentic Sharing vs. Manipulation

All communication is manipulative. The only reason we ever communicate is to manipulate our environment in some way— we communicate to get something to happen. It's why we learn to communicate in the first place: As infants, we cry (communicate) to get a drink, or a clean diaper, or some time to sleep. Nothing much nefarious about that. But somewhere between fussing until we're picked up and reading this book, most of us have come to attach negative meaning to the concept of manipulation. It's really a neutral word. Manipulation *is* negative when it is employed to get people to act against their own interests. Yet that isn't what most communication is. Being good at it, as in the strategies offered in this book, simply means you are *skillful*. The best communicators are both skillful and authentic.

It isn't always easy to remember that in a world where too many politicians, civic leaders, and religious authorities have claimed to share your values and then acted against your interests. Pardon my cynicism, but when I hear most politicians tell me they share my values, my gut reaction is, "I don't like what you're doing with them. Give them back!" People in all walks of life who have no ethical sensibility, who do not value honesty, integrity, sincerity, and authenticity, won't hesitate to use every known idea about what works in communication, every skill that makes positive relationships possible, for their own selfish interests and to their own negative ends. And there's nothing you can do about what such people choose to do with the skills and tools available to everyone.

The good news is that you have a built-in protective mechanism against this kind of manipulation: You can think for yourself.

Positive Projection

Even if you can't find any shared values, you can still click with someone by talking *as if* the shared values are there. This is called positive projection and it works because it lets people know that you recognize and appreciate their values. Even when their actions seem to indicate that they don't appreciate the values they claim. You can still tell an inconsiderate manager that you know they understand and value respect, or tell an unhelpful customer service rep that you know he can understand the importance of good service. Say, "I know you are an intelligent person, as capable of solving the problem as identifying it" or "I've seen you do this before, and I know you can do it here." Talk about it as if it is perfectly normal for him to do the kind of thing you are asking him to do. On the flip side, you can call out a negative, but say, "*It's not like you* to lash out" (or, act rashly, or choose unfairly, or gossip . . .).

When you do, you may well see the person's behavior shift. When you project a positive value on someone behaving badly, you shift her perception of herself, and chances are she will begin to behave in a way that makes that projection true. Most people rise or fall to the level of your expectations.

Furthermore, unfulfilled values or inner conflicts often lead people to negative and counterproductive emotions like explosive anger, chronic frustration, and quiet despair. Reinforce their better natures in these ways, and as they find their way back to alignment with their own values, they may be able to leave the bad behavior behind.

When Values Differ, Blend with Something Else

When you have completely different values from people with whom you'd still like to have a click, be true to your values and blend with something else. It is almost always possible to find some context for resonance. You'll only find it impossible to click if your attention is solely on the differences that divide you from someone else. Once you are on common ground, you can find more meaningful areas of common interest. In this way, you can click with just about anyone.

> You'll find it impossible to click if your attention is solely on the differences that divide you from someone else.

A limo driver in Connecticut asked me some questions as we drove to my hotel. "What are you here for?" I told him, "To give a speech." "What about?" he inquired. "How to Get People to Get You," I told him. He practically swerved off the road, as he turned around and asked me, point blank, "How do you do that!?" I told him that I knew he valued my safety (positive projection), and that he knew my safety was in his hands. Then

I told him I'd be happy to tell him the answer to his question if he promised to keep his eyes on the road while I talked. He promised, and kept his promise. Here is what I told him.

"I can see by that picture of your family on your dashboard that you love your family. And though you can't see a picture of my family, I have one with me. So you and I both value our families. And I can tell by your question that you value learning, as do I. So even though you're in the front seat and I'm in the backseat, we are both in the same car, and we have a lot in common. How do you get people to get you? Start with what you have in common.

"When we, as people, stand apart and emphasize our differences, no solution to our problems is possible, because nobody cooperates with anybody who seems to be against them. But when we find a way to stand together on some common ground, we can resolve any differences that face us, overcome any challenge that threatens us. This is what it takes for you to get me, and for me to get you. Get it?"

He got it. He recognized the value in what I was saying, and I could almost hear the click.

CHAPTER 7

Clicking Electronically

IN TODAY'S WORLD, COMMUNICATION AND CONNECTION are possible anytime, anywhere via phone, e-mail, and social networking. With so many tools for making contact and maintaining it, you might expect that it would lead to better clicking. And, in fact, it can. But these tools are sometimes just a poor substitute for real connection and genuine relationship. Used carelessly, they may block connections from going through, or even break them. Used wisely, however, they can open doors. And keep them open. There is no substitute for face-to-face interaction, but technology can create opportunities for connection that would be impossible if we were limited to communicating in person. Just remember, while a phone or computer can facilitate a connection, you are the only one who can make the click!

Click via Phone

I have three words to describe your biggest challenge on the phone: Shortened attention span. It is now possible to start, build, or ruin a relationship faster than ever. Multitasking has become a lifestyle for most people, if not everyone. E-mails arrive in a never-ending drip-drip-drip. Landlines and cell phones keep ringing. The result is that we are constantly shifting our attention with restless disinterest and following one thing only until something else comes along demanding what's left of our fractured attention.

The other hurdle you have to contend with when using the phone is that you have no visual cues. Unless you're using an Internet-based system with a camera for your calls, you won't be able to pick up on the subtle visual indicators that could help you make sense of what you're hearing, and that could help the person on the other end of the call make sense of what you're saying. That's problematic, because some people don't even know you're listening to them unless they can see you nod your head while they talk.

8 Keys to Clicking over the Phone

A phone conversation is a series of moments in which impressions are formed and decisions made. Each moment either simplifies or complicates the next moment—depending on how you handle yourself. To prevent misunderstanding and reduce conflict, it's important to maintain the basic click through frequent blending.

When building connection over the phone, you have eight key tools in your toolbox, most of which involve a form of blending. Over the phone, these tools take on even more importance and have an even greater impact than they do in person.

It's not necessary to do all of the following things in every conversation with every person. As in all matters of communication, a little bit goes a long way. You improve your chances of getting a click when you choose some aspect of the way the person you are talking with sounds and give back in the same way as you get.

1. Make sure the timing is right.

Make sure your call works as well for the person on the other end of the call as it does for you. Address the issue before bad timing becomes a barrier to clicking with a simple question: "Is this a good time to talk, or would you prefer I call back at another time?" (This is a good idea even when you are calling at a pre-appointed time.)

2. Use the person's name to hold her attention.

A person's name is a handle on her attention, and using it with greater frequency will help you to maintain the connection. This is a good way to counter people's tendency to multitask while on a call. Definitely deploy it if you are frequently asked to repeat yourself—one sign that the person you are talking to is distracted.

3. Match voice volume.

You'll find it easier to get and maintain a click if you talk at a similar volume as the person on the other end of the call.

4. Reconcile talking speed.

Speak at a similar pace as the person on the other end of the call. Fast talkers may get frustrated with slow talkers, and slow talkers may feel insulted or untrusting with fast talkers. Adopt a speed they'll be comfortable with: their own.

5. Conform your speaking rhythm to your partner's.

Some people speak in flowing sentences, one idea leading naturally to the next; others speak with gaps and hesitation. Listen for, and match, the pattern of the person you are talking to.

6. Match energy.

If a person has a subdued energy in his voice, dial yours down. Be soft-spoken and speak slowly. And when a person has a lot of energy, amp yours up!

If the person sounds down, taking your mood down a notch or two may improve her mood. If a person sounds happy, or is laughing, a similar signal from you creates the click.

7. Level vocal variety.

Use a similar variety of tones and you'll find it easier to get and maintain a click. Some people speak in a monotone or a narrowed range that leaves out the highs and lows. Some talk in a consistently high voice tone, while others in a consistently low voice tone. Some people practically sing their words. Pay attention to your tonal variety so you can use it to speak to people in familiar tones. A simple exercise to do this is to take a single sentence and repeat it with a different emphasis each time. For example, "The rain in Spain falls mainly on the plain." Then, "The rain *in* Spain falls mainly on *the* plain." Then, "The rain in *Spain* falls mainly on the *plain*." Any sentence will do. In this way, you may be able to hear the effect of vocal variety and use it to great effect with others.

8. Keep sentence length and word choices similar.
Talk using a similar sentence length and a similar complexity of word choice, and you'll find it easier to get and maintain a click. Listen for—and match—vocabulary level and variety, and use of jargon or colloquialisms or technical language (or lack thereof).

4 Ways to Click During a Phone Interview

I do phone interviews all the time. In my case, the conversations are with meeting-planners interested in hiring me for a speaking or training job, with potential clients determining if I'm the right coach for them, and with radio and television producers either curious to know if I'm right for their shows or hosts interviewing me on the show. The interview is a pivotal moment, a limited opportunity to make an important connection that can really impact your life. Here are a few things you can do to increase your chances for clicking during a phone interview.

1. Use a landline.
In a cell phone world, this small detail can still make a difference. The last thing you need is for your call to get dropped, or

disrupted by static. If you don't have one of your own, find someone who does and ask if you can use her space for your conversation. Friends typically say yes to this kind of request. There are business centers in many cities, even in airports, where you can use a landline for a very small charge. Trust me, it's worth every penny.

2. Be prepared.

Before you even answer (or dial) the phone, get your head in the game by thinking about what you know and don't know about the organization. Come up with at least three to five talking points you want to make to create the right impression. These talking points should be brief statements that you want to introduce into the mind of the interviewer—and make sure to practice them in advance. If you are asked a question that you can't answer, you'll at least be able to make one of these points and keep the interview on track. A word of advice: Make sure those points are about what you have to offer, not what you need.

The other half of being prepared is to create a zone around you that can keep out all potential interruptions. Have whatever you might need (water, notepad, calendar . . .) within reach.

3. Hold the focus.

No multitasking allowed! Holding a singular focus on the task at hand sends a powerful signal that you consider the call to be of the utmost importance. Be respectful about your interviewer's time.

If the call comes unexpectedly, ask for a moment to get yourself together. You can say that the call is important to you, and you need to go to another room so you won't be distracted. If you keep the delay to a minimum, you will actually sound better than if you just started the interview right after answering the phone.

If you're taking notes while the interviewer is talking, make sure to tell the interviewer, so he doesn't wonder about any silence on your end of the line. That message may also come across as a statement of commitment, and thus works in your favor.

4. Listen and blend.

Remember to apply connected listening to whatever is said. Don't wait to be told what something means. Actively ask questions about any information offered to you to find out whatever details you can.

If the interviewer doesn't respond after you've answered a question, turn the question around. If you've been asked what makes you the right candidate for the job, and your answer is greeted with silence, ask "What qualities do you hope to find that make someone right for this position?"

Take your cues from the interviewer and then use some of the eight blending methods described earlier in this chapter. If your interviewer makes small talk, follow her lead and speak to her need by adjusting your style. Likewise, if she is strictly business, you should be too. Match energy, mood, and all the rest.

Click Using E-mail

E-mail can be used to get a basic click with someone or to set the stage for clicking the old-fashioned way. E-mail can also support a deeper click established in person and maintained over time, but it's next to impossible to create a deep or lasting click with e-mail alone. I'm not saying it can't ever be done, but the elements of time, space, and words just don't add up to much of a connection, no matter how good the intentions are. Use this tool the wrong way and you risk losing a chance to click again. You do need to know how to communicate powerfully in writing via e-mail, but you also need to know when to take your relationship offline and make time for a personal click.

E-mail is a powerful way to attend to specific kinds of messages. For example, e-mail can get the ball rolling when you want to make contact with someone you don't know. (Just be sure to do it in a way that inclines him to want to know you!) You can use it for scheduling by sending calendar items to either be accepted or declined. You can use e-mail for setting the table for meetings, by providing background or need-to-know information ahead of time. You can use e-mail for the exchange of ideas, to work through details and keep a running log. E-mail can help you keep in touch after an in-person click has been established, and in established relationships where in-person contact isn't always feasible. For everything else, there are likely to be better ways to make a connection.

The Challenges of E-mail

We face three main challenges with e-mail when our goal is to build, or at least not undermine, relationships.

The first is the sheer volume of e-mail we receive (and send), which makes it a huge challenge for anyone trying to get anything done. The ease with which we can compose and send an e-mail has led to difficulty in managing the flow of it, and warmth and friendliness often take a backseat to the business at hand. Unless it's in a message between friends or associates who have a friendly relationship, people just don't have much time or tolerance for off-topic questions like, "How are you, what's new?" that might get a moment in the spotlight in person or over the phone.

The ease of sending an e-mail creates the second challenge too: The ability to respond in haste, or to copy and paste with little effort, introduces the peril of sending off a message before you have a chance to think better of it. Hit Reply, say what's on your mind, press Send, and suddenly there is no going back.

Finally, because e-mail is text-based, it lacks the vocal and facial cues and the emotional texture, that illuminate what words mean when we use them in speaking to one another in person. So it can be difficult to accurately interpret what you read when you get a message. It can be hard to tell if someone is being friendly or demanding, feeling frustrated or angry, joking or just being direct. Furthermore, your mood is likely to dictate your response to a message. Whatever the writer's meaning, it can be twisted because the reader is having a bad day, or is distracted, or experiences a blood sugar drop. Or any of a hundred other negative influences. And if someone is in a sorry state while composing a message, he may actually pass it along with his message.

Emoting over E-mail

Cornell professor of communication Jeff Hancock recently published a study demonstrating how people's moods show through in the messages they send via e-mail, and instant and text messaging. People who were sad, anxious, or frustrated while composing their thoughts sent fewer, shorter messages, and used more words related to those emotions (*annoyed*, *disappointed*, and so on). They expressed less encouragement and less agreement. And their feelings came through loud and clear—so much so, in fact, that they were "contagious"— the receivers tended to begin to feel the same way.

---

8 Ways to Make E-mail Messages Work

E-mail isn't the best form of communication for every purpose, but it certainly has its place. Much of what works to click in person also works to click electronically, even when you have only the words to rely on. But you have to take its limitations into account and you have to use it wisely. The exception is with close friends and family members, who won't much care how you say what you say, because they already know and love you, and love hearing from you. With everyone else, heed these suggestions to build better connections.

1. Be polite.

This is the first rule of all written correspondence, not just e-mail. My mom used to say that you get more flies with honey than with vinegar. And though there's so little time for social pleasantries these days, the best e-mails contain some basic socially friendly features. A pleasant introduction (just like you would have in a real letter) like "Dear _____," sets a positive first impression. Lines of positive thought can be a plus, since they signal your friendly intentions, like, "Hello," or "I hope all is well in your world."

Equally, end a message with some more general pleasantries, such as "Thank you for your time. Sincerely, _____" or "I look forward to your reply. Best wishes," to leave a positive impression behind.

2. Use the subject line.

The subject line tells people what they are getting into before they get into it. A blank subject line says that what you have to say must not be very important. A lost subject, which is what happens when you leave out the subject, or it gets moved out of the way when forwarding takes place a few too many times (Re: Re: Re: Re: Re: Re: Re: What?) tells your recipient that the e-mail isn't personal. Instead, give a short descriptive subject line to get attention for your message.

When an e-mail conversation begins, the subject line states what it's about. But in the back and forth of e-mail, the topic may evolve (or devolve) into something else entirely. Let this go on too long, and the purpose of responding to you may no longer be obvious to your recipient. Keeping the subject line up to date with the content of the conversation will help you create a more consistent connection.

3. Keep it brief.

Respect the other person's time and effort by keeping it short and simple, making your point obvious, and asking for what you want. That's good for your recipient, so it's good for your relationship with the recipient. When a person opens an e-mail, it is just one of many, another thing to respond to, not something to spend time with. That's why e-mail is great for brief interactions. The longer the e-mail, the less attention it is likely to receive—and the less likely to is to produce a click.

4. Frame your message.

E-mails are single-shot opportunities to make your point, ask your question, or produce a result. To do that, you need to carefully frame your written communication so that your recipient can zero in on exactly what you have to say or want to have happen.

There are three steps to delivering a simple, direct, and effective message:

• Give your recipient a reason to keep reading. Right up front, state your intention. "The reason I'm sending this to you is to give you information to prepare for our next meeting," or "I'm writing to give you an update on our last conversation." This opening line sets the table for all that follows.

• Give your recipient a call for action. Here, you tell her what you want her to do as a result of reading what follows. "I'd like to hear back from you regarding how this information impacts our plan," or "Please share what I am about to tell you with the rest of your team, so we are all on the same page," or "I'm eager to get your recommendations based on this information." There are times when no response or action is required. In that case, tell him. A simple way to indicate this is to open your message with an "FYI" (for your information), as in, "FYI, here's a summary of our recent phone call. I hope you find it helpful."

• Third, and finally: Give your recipient the information, keeping it clear and concise.

5. Put out any flames.

Emotional language in an e-mail can be risky. If you're having strong feelings while writing an e-mail, or even while you're reading an e-mail, your message is likely to trigger unintended consequences. That's an e-mail "flame," and it's lit by any message that triggers an emotional reaction. The problem with flames is they spread. You send a flame, you get one back, and before you know it, your entire relationship is ablaze in misunderstanding.

Make time your ally. There's no good reason to respond immediately when you're having a negative reaction. Wait until you've clarified your message and managed your emotions before you respond, finding a positive frame of reference to build up the relationship instead of tearing it down. Never, ever reply to an e-mail impulsively. Take some time to collect your thoughts before putting them into sensible (and send-able) writing.

6. Only send to groups with permission.

Think twice before sending a group e-mail. Impersonal e-mails are easily disregarded (and discarded) by the recipient. Unwanted e-mail is even worse; it not only clogs in-boxes, but also downgrades the value of all e-mail.

7. When sending to groups, keep addresses private.

Protect the privacy of all your e-mail contacts by hiding everyone's e-mail address when you are sending a message to long lists of multiple recipients. In most systems, this is simply a matter of putting e-mail addresses in the "bcc:" field when sending to a list. (Good netiquette requires stripping addresses out of the body of an e-mail as well.) Omitting this basic sign of respect for someone's privacy shows a degree of disconnect between your actions and their possible consequences, and could block a potential click.

The only time everyone's addresses may be appropriate in a group e-mail is when the group is a team working together on a specific project, where each member needs to be in on what every member is saying to other members.

8. Watch the funny stuff.

A little kidding goes a long way. That's *if* the other person gets the joke. Unless you already know your recipient's sense of humor, you're probably better off avoiding jokes altogether. Always think carefully before you send along any of the plethora of online opportunities for fun—humorous lists, zany video clips, funny pictures. It's a dicey proposition to send these things to people who haven't asked for them. Each "fluff" message you send can dilute the value to your recipient of other messages you send, so when in doubt, leave it out.

How to Click Using Social Networks

Love them or hate them, social networks are here to stay. They allow us to begin relationships with people we otherwise might never meet, and make public connections that otherwise would remain invisible. Moreover, they permit us to reconnect across time and space, giving families and communities a common meeting place, and potential business partners a chance to find and cement business relationships.

Social networks are the new tribes. Belonging is a matter of registering and creating a profile or a page, and making or finding "friends" or "followers."

Whether it's Facebook, Twitter, LinkedIn, Plaxo, or Ning, or one of the thousands of other networks organized around a single activity or industry, social networks make it possible to connect over time and space, and to make new connections in far less time than ever before.

It used to be that if you wanted to know about a book or a movie, you would ask around until you found someone with an opinion. Nowadays, opinions are everywhere, and people love to share them. Thanks to social networks, you can easily find people to discuss a favorite TV show, share photos of your recent trip through the Amazon rain forest, or watch videos of your kid's school play. You can put the most personal parts of your life out on networks for everyone to see. You can learn from the brightest minds. And you can witness the witlessness of foolish people's private lives.

All Networks Serve to Help People Click

The purpose of networks is to bring people together, but not all networks accomplish this in the same way. Every network has a distinct purpose. While some are designed for matchmaking or music sharing, or customer support, others are designed to maintain social connections with friends, and build relationships. Networks like LinkedIn, Facebook, and MySpace build strength on expansion. In our far-flung society, where people are constantly on the move, online networking makes keeping in touch as simple as the click of a mouse. But if you prefer keeping your connections close, it is likely that there is a local network in your area. In my area, the local newspaper provides just such a network. Or you can just start a local group on a larger network, like Ning.com. These kinds of social networks leverage the power of the whole network for word-of-mouth advertising, so they are great for political candidates, artist branding, and event promotion.

It's the nature of these networks to grow. If you have ten friends, and each of your friends has ten friends, it doesn't take long to have a personal network of thousands of people who are potential business partners, sources of local information, and resources when you need them. Though the networks may be separate from each other now, the borders between them are quickly coming down. One day, instead of searching through pages, you'll be able to search for people that meet your criteria. When you have something to sell, you'll post an ad and people looking for that type of item will be told about it automatically from across all the networks.

But we're not there yet. There are still a few technical and personal barriers to deal with. Chief among the personal obstacles is that social networking, while more time-efficient than the in-person variety, does require an investment of time, and most people are pressed for time. Some people try it out and then leave it when the novelty wears off. Those who find it worthwhile to stay with it eventually learn to build it into their daily routine, and allow it only so much time. Another problem is that getting to know people online doesn't always give you the same real life knowledge that personal contact does. Without vocal cues, our online experience is shaped by words and pictures, all of which can be manipulated to create false fronts and potentially open us up to yet more unsolicited messages.

To compensate, networkers learn a developing code for their words-only communication. Bad behavior gets tagged, and those who engage in it are isolated, un-followed, and locked out of participation. Get labeled a spammer (someone who sends unsolicited commercial messages) or a splogger (someone who posts specious blog posts and comments just to create links to commercial endeavors) and you wind up alone, despised, and maybe even having your access taken away.

The Online Democracy

Online social networks democratize relationships. To a certain extent, it no longer matters what position you hold in a company, how old you are, what you look like, or how cool you are. People online are less likely to judge you on external characteristics than if they met you face-to-face. In a way, you are who you say you are. People put themselves out to the network either as they see themselves, or, perhaps more importantly, as they wish to be seen. It's not uncommon for people to use fake degrees, for example, or to inflate their résumé to make something weak look stronger, or simply to describe themselves as older than they are, or younger, or more competent. So it helps if others will back you up on your claims through referrals and testimonials.

In an online social network, people you would otherwise never meet or whom you wouldn't necessarily want to spend time with in real life, can become valuable additions to your network, increasing your apparent popularity because of the network of connections they bring. When I comment on my associate Kare's post, for example, it becomes visible to my followers and connections, who may then comment on her post as well. My comment becomes an introduction to Kare to people who otherwise might never meet her.

With so many strangers having access to you, could a few rotten apples spoil the whole barrel? Not really. It's easy enough to remove people, un-follow them, block their e-mails, and mute their presence. People only stay in your network if you agree to have them there.

Some networks, such as LinkedIn and Plaxo, are designed specifically to facilitate business. In this case, every connection you open yourself up to increases the number of potential business partners and service providers available to you, while making your products and services available to more and more people. If you accept a connection to someone you don't know, there may be no immediate advantage, but it could happen that someone will find out about you by clicking through someone she knows quite well. I've gotten business requests this way, and it's always a delightful surprise.

Your value *to* the network is related to the value *of* your network. Think about it! Your network is valuable to the extent that it contains a whole host of people with a variety of skills, resources, contacts, ideas, and opportunities. Add that value together, and it's a small community of people capable of great things. While chances are that they are not all working on the same things, each person in turn has something to offer to other communities. The more people you bring through your own connections, the greater your worth to the larger network.

> Your value *to* the network is related to
> the value *of* your network.

Connecting with people you don't know who are connected to people you do know requires a careful dance. If you ask to be added as a friend without an introduction, the person seeking quality in his network is likely to decline. If you ask for someone's business merely because he is on the same network as you, the odds are good that your offer will be declined. Just because someone puts her life online in a social network does not mean she is inclined to respond positively to whatever comes her way via the Internet.

So, offline or on, you need to build a relationship before you can do much with it. And online as well as off-, this starts with a click. In the most basic ways, relationships are developed online much as they are offline. Jeff Hancock, the communications professor at Cornell, demonstrated this in a study where participants who didn't know one another were paired up and instructed to get their partners to like them—through a brief IM conversation. One group of participants had access to their partner's Facebook profile while the other was flying/typing blind.

Who do you think did better? Those who could use tidbits picked up on Facebook to ask questions and mention information that aligned with the other person's interests. We like people who are like us. And we know it—so in getting someone to like us, it's a card we play quite naturally. In fact, the more the participants used those kinds of questions, and the more they dropped in pertinent information, the more their partners liked them.

Let's say that I know Chris, and Chris knows Dave, and Dave knows Alison. Alison is a graphic designer, and I have a marketing piece that needs help. Because each of them has made their network visible, it would appear that I can bypass Chris and Dave entirely, and go directly to Alison. Next thing you know, I'm sending a message to Alison across the social network. It's the equivalent of a cold call. "Hello Alison, I see that you know Dave, who is friends with my friend Chris. I also see that you're a graphic designer. I've looked at some of your work, and I wonder if you would consider helping me with a marketing piece?" Chances are that such an approach will produce the same kind of result as you would get in the offline world: Some will respond positively; some won't. Alison may be intrigued, or looking for work. Or, she might be busy, and have no time for a stranger. In that case, you'd be wise to adopt the stance of okay, so what, and either find someone else who might be interested or do what you could have done in the first place: ask Chris to introduce you to Dave, then ask Dave to introduce you to Alison.

However, you might be able to increase your chances of success while cutting out the contacts in between if you use the other person's profile to help you structure an "ethical bribe" to get some attention. An ethical bribe is an incentive technique that is common online and offline too. When Amazon offers you free shipping, that's a bribe to take action. When the family at the farmer's market offers you a goat cheese sample, that's a bribe to consider buying more of it. Simply, it's giving people an incentive to take some kind of action. And for our purposes, that action is to respond to your request for contact.

Ideally, what you offer doesn't cost you much, or anything, but has value to the person whose contact you desire. This could be as simple as a link, or an interview request. Several people I know who do radio shows tell me they started out wanting to meet people they admired. Asking for an interview almost always got them a yes. That interview offer was an ethical bribe, because the people they admired were interested in the publicity.

You might offer to support a cause cherished by your potential contact in exchange for some of his time, or promote a project that he values. You can often find such information by reading the profile posted by the person inside the social network. "My name is Rick Kirschner, and I'd like to blog about the great work of the Open Space group you mentioned. Can we set up a phone call to discuss that work, along with some of my ideas for how we can work together going forward? You can read my profile and learn more about me at this link. Interested? Please reply." For the price of perhaps just providing a little time or information, you can offer to do something that matters to the person and potentially interest her in something that matters to you.

On the other hand, you may notice that the person shares some of your values, and put them forward as the common ground on which to explore whether working together would be a good fit. "I worked on so-and-so's campaign in the last election, and enjoyed the chance to inform people about the healthcare issue and how it affects all of us. If you're of a like mind about this issue, would you be interested in talking about the possibility of doing some work together?" or "I'm active in the conservation movement, and I'm working on a marketing piece aimed at educating people about that cause. If this is something that also interests you, would you be willing to talk with me about it?"

Increase Your Chances of Connecting

Along with adding someone as a friend, or posting your own goings-on, you can enhance your online clickability in the following ways:

• Ask for a recommendation.

A testimonial about you from anyone other than you says more about you than anything you can say about yourself. Let's say that Chris has done work with me and holds my work in high esteem. He can post his opinion on my page, and anyone that visits my page to check me out can see that opinion and use it in forming her own.

• Ask for a referral.

Social networking lets you see who the people you know, know. If you want to talk to someone who is connected to one or more of your connections, you ask your connection to put in a good word for you, either directly or on your profile.

• Recommend someone else.

Go to the page of someone whose business you want to support, and leave a testimonial about the work she does. Oftentimes that'll get you a little "I'll scratch your back, you scratch mine" response, but even if you don't you'll be building goodwill. In my experience, people who are generous in their recommendations are abundant in the recommendations of others as well.

• Make a referral.

Let's say that you know a meeting planner at a company that would benefit from Chris's work. You can direct him to Chris's page and mention something along the lines of "Hope you're well. Thought this might be useful!" This gives you a reason to stay connected with your initial contact while helping another person in your network.

- **Make a new connection.**

You can make direct contact with anyone that is connected to your network. To click with strangers, follow the rules of social networking (following) so you attract rather than put off your target. You can't click if they just ignore you!

5 Rules for Networking on Social Networks

The social networking system has an irresistible pull for people who see its potential. It can be tempting to jump in and try to make everything happen at once. Resist that temptation. It's not only unnecessary, but also unwise. You've got to learn your way around first. Observe how others behave. Be wise about what you do, what you say, and how you engage with people. From the moment you begin to connect with others, your on-line history will forever be a part of your online identity.

1. Don't spam your network.

The fastest way to keep a connection from happening is to try selling your ideas, products, or services to people who don't know you. That's likely to be perceived, rightly, as spam. Better to click first and then introduce your services and products later.

Case in point: You sign up with Ecademy, an international business network. Some people see that you've signed up, and they say hello. Some see you are new to the network and offer help. Some, seeing that you're new, offer you membership in a group organized around a theme related to your profile. All of these are opportunities for you to click.

On the other hand, some go straight to the pitch. I don't know about you, but I don't have the time or interest to hear someone pitching her business to me if I don't know her first. All business is about relationships first, and that means getting a click before making a pitch.

2. Don't be a stranger.

Learn something before saying something. Tell people how you found them, or find out how they found you. Make the connection interesting. Avoid using generic introductions such as, "Hi, I found you and thought your résumé was interesting." Strangers talk in such big generalizations. Friends are more personal, and able to be more specific because of the values, motivations, or background they share. Find something personal around which to connect. Everything you need to know is in the person's profile.

Consider the examples of two people who made contact with me through a business network I joined. Each person was interested in doing business, but one introduction was intriguing while the other was off-putting:

Hello Rick:

I am interested in networking with you. I'm in the business of setting up people with Nevada corporations to run their new businesses while achieving the utmost in tax savings. I offer them several of my vendors' services to continue growing their business.

I look forward to hearing from you.

Best regards, Sandy

And:

Hi Rick,

My tax consulting business works with many companies going through change. I read several of your blog posts, and now I'm curious to know more about your opinion on what it takes to make positive change. I guess what I'm asking is, what's your business the Art of Change all about for you?

Warm Regards,

Nadia

When I received Sandy's message, her offer had nothing to do with me or my business, and I had no interest in responding. When I received Nadia's message, I was intrigued. There was no sales pitch, just a curiosity to know more. That was an opening, the beginning of a conversation. Only after we had exchanged a few messages inside the social network did Nadia raise the subject of her business and how it might benefit me. At that point, it didn't bother me. In fact, I felt she had my genuine interests in mind. Many people like to talk about themselves and the things they care about, and if you ask them to do so, you will build a connection.

Be warned, however. If you're not really interested, your outreach won't have the same effect. Nobody likes being used or deceived. People helping people is what business is all about, and most people understand that when you're in business, you're trying to grow it whenever opportunity presents itself.

Only in a caring and connected communication can the real opportunity become obvious.

3. You get out what you put in.
The more you maintain an online presence, the more likely you are to gain recognition and make connections with valuable allies and friends.

One of the best networkers and collaborative business people I know is Kare Anderson, of the Say It Better Center in San Francisco. Kare regularly posts resources, stories, and suggestions on her LinkedIn and Facebook pages. She participates. She has made herself a valuable online resource, and when people log in to check their personal pages, my guess is that more than a few check into Kare's pages shortly thereafter.

4. Instead of asking for something, offer something.
And I'm not talking about a free sample, either. Tell the network what you bring to it, whether it is knowledge, ability, or connections. Post it in your profile. Write an article about it. In this way, you can make what is valuable about you to your own network available to the larger network.

5. Take it slow.
Online networks take time. Rushing into connections and demanding instant gratification is annoying and adds pressure to an already pressure-cooked world. Electronic communication happens at the speed of electrons, but human beings don't move quite so fast when it comes to relationship-building.

Think of time as an ally. Take as much of it as you need to build a real connection before trying to get someone to click with your business or idea.

Technology has truly created a World Wide Web, connecting us in ways unimaginable in the not-so-distant past. Careful use of the strands that link us supports and strengthens not just the person-to-person connection, but also the forces that keep us together. *Click.*

CHAPTER 8

Troubleshooting

WHETHER IT'S A MANAGER PUTTING DOWN AN EMPLOYEE, a parent yelling at a child, or two strangers being snarky and disagreeable over something that changes nothing, bad behavior is the single biggest obstacle to good relationships. I've received too many e-mails and questions to count from desperate people wanting to know what to do when trouble strikes and bad feelings take the place of positive interactions. Take this one, for example:

> Dear Dr. K,
> I'm having a terrible time dealing with a consultant in my office. He loves control, threatens people with his potential anger. He's accusatory, self-righteous, condescending, scolding, with a soupçon of whining and guilt-tripping. Everything must be locked down according to his plan before he's willing to move forward. There's very little "give." He's good at the organizational side of his work, and a real team player as long as he runs the team. He thinks he's in charge even though he's not, but he often gets control by coming on like the expert. Any suggestions?
> George

When the click isn't happening, it's time to troubleshoot. Identify what's going on, how you're reacting to it, and what's likely to turn it around. Take this opportunity to turn personal problems into personal relationships.

Turn personal problems into personal relationships.

The most common conflicts that make clicking impossible fall into five categories:

- Strong opinions, where people disagree with each other and are committed to defending their differences;
- Meddling, where one person makes it her business to interfere in the other person's business;
- Gossip, where one person speaks in an unflattering way about another person and the comments get back to the person being gossiped about;
- Unconstructive criticism, where pointing out short-comings and personal failings allows one person to feel superior to another; and
- Sarcasm, where hurtful remarks get hidden behind smiles and inside seemingly innocuous statements.

Rule #1: It's Not About You

Relationships are personal, but bad behavior is not. The real trouble begins when you take bad behavior personally.

When negative behavior is directed at you, remind yourself that *it is not about you*. More often than not, it *is* about the other person stressing out and lacking the resources to deal effectively with some circumstance in his own life.

Criticism is a classic example. When someone starts pointing out your shortcomings and highlighting them as examples of deeper failings, you can almost always trace it back to one of two things: Either he is in a bad mood and you happened to get in his way, or he dislikes something that you do that he himself does and is oblivious to (like talking too much, not listening, and the like).

Take this opportunity to learn from the other person. Listen for real concerns or for a reality check. It is imperative that you distinguish between difficult behavior and the person engaged in it. You'll be more able to find your way to a click. With anyone.

Rule #2: Ask Yourself if It *Could* Be About You

Because, let's face it, sometimes it is. As you read in George's letter, what you do can start a fire or fan the flames. Instead of focusing all your attention on what the other person is doing wrong, try to see what you are doing to worsen the situation. Taking responsibility for an issue can be the most proactive solution.

Question the assumptions you've applied to the other person and ask yourself if they're accurate. For example, how do you know someone "loves control"? If you think someone is disrespectful, what do you base this on? Could it mean something else? Blame is often about projection. What's frustrating you might be something that you need to change within. It's a good idea to observe how what you're saying, thinking, and believing about the other person might actually be true about you.

Ask yourself what you want. This is the time to identify your desired outcome, or how you want to impact the relationship in this particular situation. It's impossible to solve a problem if you only know what you don't want. Then consider how you want to respond to this behavior, what you want to tell yourself about it that encourages rather than discourages you, and what you want to feel about the person as you interact with her.

When George, who wrote me about his problems with the consultant in his office, applied these principles, he was able to resolve his issue. He wrote again a week later to follow up:

Dear Dr. K,

Well, the republic is saved. I had an excellent conversation with my colleague, which resulted in part in my owning up to how I contributed to the problem in the first place, and his acknowledging the inappropriateness of his response. All's well.

But more. Encouraged by your suggestions, I tried to see what had upset me in this confrontation. And from that I learned a tremendous lesson about my own

tendency to fix on a position and defend it. Happily, it is
only situational. So thanks. I can take it from here.
   George

8 Ways to Resolve Trouble with Positions

A position is an opinion stated as a fact. Everyone has positions, and when someone is defending his position too strongly,
it is extremely difficult to create a click. Even when the positions are of critical importance, there are several options that
can break through the impasse and even lead to a click.

1. Acknowledge his importance.

Some people defend their positions because it makes them feel
important. Recognizing the importance of someone's position,
will show that you recognize *his* importance. "I can see this
matters to you greatly." "I can tell this is something you care
about." "You've clearly spent a great deal of time thinking about
this." People will be much more likely to work out a problem if
they feel valued.

2. Find a way to agree.

One of the simplest ways to agree with someone is to break
down a disagreement into smaller pieces. Find points where
you both can agree. Narrowing an area of disagreement has
the inverse effect of increasing the areas of agreement.

    That's exactly what one of my clients did when the board of
directors she served on was bogged down in a disagreement

over whether or not to continue an official relationship with another organization. Betsy aimed to narrow the differences between the board members by making explicit the areas of agreement, and identifying components of the disagreement not in question. With Betsy's encouragement, the board members realized they all agreed that the other organization's work was worthy—and that their own organization needed to work efficiently in similar areas. From there, it was much easier and less overwhelming to talk about joining forces to accomplish their goal, and work through to a joint decision.

3. Respond favorably to the fact that he is speaking up.

Even when you disagree with a stated position, you may be able to come to agreement by acknowledging his willingness to state his case: "While I disagree with what you propose, I'm glad you spoke up. We need to address this." Speak directly and with respect, and in return you will receive respect for taking *your* stand. This is especially effective when someone is expressing a strong position because no one else is, and he feels obligated to make the point. ("If nobody else is going to say it, I will!")

4. Don't back away.

To a person defending a strong position, backing off might look like a signal of weakness. The message it sends is that either you are intimidated, which won't win you points with anyone, or you don't have the courage of your convictions, which undermines the value of whatever else you say. You'll do better to simply hold your ground. This is not the time to move forward, but you should stay where you are as you hear the other person out, and as you respond. This conveys mutuality and commands respect.

5. Don't be pulled into an argument.

Arguments make clicking ever harder. Engaging discussion is a form of blending that will help you click with a person who enjoys the give-and-take. Be careful in strongly defending your own position. If you are too defensive, you will create an impasse.

If you do feel the need to explain yourself, ask if she's interested in your opinion. "There's something I don't think I've expressed clearly. Will you hear me out?" Opening yourself to her opinion shows you care.

6. Buy some time.

When there's no compelling reason to respond to a strong position right away, your best choice may be to call time out. Give the person time to reconsider or discover an error in his own thinking. More importantly, with time, you may learn a little more before you talk about the issue again, which will help you to have a more positive interaction.

Arguing for Argument's Sake

Some people express strong positions because they are looking for a good argument.

Marvin is, as he describes himself, an opinionated SOB. He's not at all embarrassed by the fact that people cower when he gets worked up. The few brave enough to talk back are easily shouted down. When Marvin speaks, he speaks with *certainty*—whether he knows what he's talking about or not!

Bill worked in the same office as Marvin, and their paths frequently crossed. Despite Marvin's demeanor, Bill honestly saw a lot that he liked: Marvin said what he thought, was always and above all very direct. He liked that he could count on Marvin for the honest truth. Yet most of the time, their interactions were disagreements, point and counterpoint. Bill decided the only way to get into Marvin's head was to cater to his argumentative behavior.

Marvin had been a PC user for years, knew a lot about programming, and hated anything from Apple. Bill was an Apple fan, and like most Apple fans, couldn't understand how anyone in his right mind could prefer a PC.

Whenever Marvin said something insulting, demeaning, or just plain mean about Bill and his love for Macs, Bill would go back and forth a bit, just for the sake of giving Marvin the pleasure of engaging in battle. But Bill never set out to *win*, he just used this to stay in the game.

After a couple of rounds, Bill would say, "Well, maybe you're right, time will tell." And he meant it. He figured that given time, technology would ripen and the facts would speak for themselves. From that point on, he would refuse to say anything more about it. Until the next time Marvin tried to start it up.

One day, Marvin's kids talked him into buying an iPod. It didn't take him long to appreciate how well it worked. Soon, he was reaching out to Bill to tell him what a great piece of technology it was and how it had changed everything for him. Bill let him go on, just nodding and enjoying his quiet victory. When Apple came out with a new computer, Marvin would begrudgingly say, "Well, I have to admit, it's pretty cool." It had taken a little time, but Bill and Marvin developed a new pattern of laughing, talking and enjoying an honest and direct relationship. *Click.*

7. Get more information.

Assume you don't know what the opinionated person means or why his position matters to him. Just ask him to tell you more about it, not generally but specifically. Find out everything you can about the position using your listening skills. Find out the values that make someone's position important, then acknowledge them and talk about how you share them if you can. Find out his motivation for taking the position, and speak to that when you respond.

A Fresh Set of Eyes

Eddie was driving his team crazy. Hot-headed and opinionated, whenever he felt frustrated, he had a bad habit of snapping at anyone who disagreed with his positions.

The situation deteriorated as each person's behavior became increasingly automatic and unproductive.

When Margy got assigned to the team, it didn't take her long to observe Eddie's behavior for herself. It soon became obvious to her, perhaps because she was new to the situation, that Eddie's lashing out was related to his backing himself into a corner with his own positions. She also noticed that her other teammates only fed his frustration by shouting back at him or shutting down around him.

The next time Eddie started to lose it during a meeting, Margy was ready to step in. After he shouted, "You're not listening! This plan is a major mistake, and it doesn't take into account . . ." she interjected with, "Eddie, help me understand what you're saying. Maybe you're on to something, but I'm not alone in not getting it. Help me out." The more she asked, the calmer he became. And it turned out that some of what he said actually made a lot of sense, when he could present it calmly. And Eddie, his brain now connected to his mouth, was receptive when Margy offered her own insights to either add to his idea or change it for the better.

Eddie responded to the opportunity to get his position out all at once. He was able to learn more about his own position by talking about it to a receptive audience, and the team learned from Margy's example what they needed to do to deal with him. *Click*.

8. Get others involved.

When a position sounds like a personal attack, try to deperson-
alize it. Draw others into the conversation. It's not uncommon
for someone else to hear or see something that you've missed.
By inviting other people into the discussion, you increase the
chances of gathering more useful information, while diluting
the possible impact of the position.

4 Ways to Handle Trouble with Criticism

If you're like most people, you hate being criticized. And, like
most people, you probably have a well developed knee-jerk reaction anytime criticism is leveled at you, particularly when you
know the person is wrong. The trouble is, that won't help you
click. Try these strategies instead:

1. Help him criticize you.

The best thing to do when someone starts to criticize you is
help him. Draw him out. Gather information. Ask him to be as
specific as possible.

I know this is counterintuitive, but it works. There are only
three reasons why people criticize other people: They have
legitimate feedback; they're having a bad day and you got in
the way; or they know you hate it, and do it to get a rise out
of you.

In every case, the same approach can defuse the criticism.
In the first instance, where someone has an honest message for
you, asking for more allows him to be straight with you and

allows you to gain useful information. Say, for example, your boss tells you that your proposal was disorganized. Ask for the details and thank him for the critique. Take his feedback and apply it to improve your performance on the next proposal you write.

In the second scenario, where someone is simply having a horrible day, chances are the criticism has nothing to do with you. Asking her to talk about her rotten mood—and what caused it—may help her realize whatever is bothering her isn't your fault. She may even apologize. If your coworker accuses you of not really caring about her work, or your joint project, resist the urge to defend yourself. Ask her for help in understanding her point. Your question will demonstrate that you care. But in any similar situation, asking for details provides a moment of reflection, and you are likely to hear something along the lines of, "Oh, it's not really you. I'm just having one of those days!"

Lastly, if someone is simply trying to get a rise out of you, gathering information will take all the fun out of criticizing you, and she will either stop or find a different target to provoke. If your client says you really know how to take the long way around even when things have been proceeding apace, ask, "What is the long way?" Whatever her answer, ask for more details, until the client realizes you just are not taking the bait and gives up. You don't necessarily click with the person, but at least you can put an end to the criticism. And you just might set in motion a click with any witnesses impressed with the cool way you handle the heat.

2. Say thank you.

Listen to the criticism and say, "Thank you." Thank her for being honest with you, for bringing the issue to your attention, or just thank her for caring. Then let it go.

When you defend yourself against undeserved criticism, you make yourself look guiltier than if you had said nothing at all. Turn the tables on the person, demonstrate civil behavior, and signal your ability to be tactful and respectful. This ends the criticism in the moment, and has the added benefit of making you less of a target for criticism in the long run.

3. Accept what's valid about criticism.

Sometimes, criticism is the ugly wrapping on a valuable gift. While it may be difficult to receive that gift, it is your best option for building a relationship and improving whatever needs fixing.

Let people know that you've heard the valid part of their criticism by apologizing. Your apology should come from the heart and have no conditions attached. Instead of, "I apologize, but I had my reasons," which turns the apology into what sounds like an excuse, all you have to say is "I'm sorry for how this affected you." You may find their reciprocal offer of forgiveness is a doorway to connection.

I had been asked at a company-sponsored costume party to announce the awards for best costume, worst costume, etc. Just before I went up onstage to give the awards, the VP of the company asked me to give an unannounced award for the "sexiest" costume, and who to give it to. I did as I was asked, and didn't think any more about it.

Not until the end of the event, when I was confronted by an attendee who was deeply offended. She proceeded to accuse me of callous and base motives, and called me every name in the book. And I, of course, defended myself, because I was just doing what I'd been asked. I tried telling my side, but she'd have none of it.

It wasn't until it was all over that it dawned on me: I should simply have responded, "Clearly I offended you. And I am deeply sorry. That wasn't my intent. Thank you for telling me how you feel."

I sought her out at the next morning's breakfast with this new, improved approach. I walked straight up to her and apologized. "You were honest with me about something, and I didn't hear you out. I apologize for that, and for having offended you, too. I hope you'll give me a second chance." I started to walk away and she stopped me. "I'm already over it. But it means a lot to me that you get it. Thank you." *Click.*

4. Ask for a retrial.

Nobody likes to hear negative opinions about themselves, but not all negative feedback needs to be taken as a sign of trouble. There's nothing wrong in someone making an objective assessment of your performance. In fact, prudence can save a lot of time, money, energy, and pointlessness in relationships. Getting feedback is helpful to anyone seeking to do better.

Trouble begins when someone starts expressing negative opinions about how you have somehow failed to measure up to some unknown or unstated measure of perfection. A judgmental person can render an opinion of you that you've never asked for, gavel you down if you try to argue in your own defense, or dismiss your case before you've had a chance to make it.

It's natural to try and avoid crossing swords or crossing paths with people who do this. Who wants to be judged or have their motives questioned and their issues ignored?

If you say nothing, you create the impression that they must be right because you have no defense. And if you defend yourself, you look guilty as charged.

Here's a better choice: Gather up your courage, ask a few questions, thank him for his "feedback," and then ask him what it will take to change his mind about you. Asking for a retrial changes the dynamic of the relationship. Backtrack what he says, provide him with the evidence he says he needs to change his opinion, and the case is closed. That is the moment of click.

Two months ago, Joan went through a personal crisis that severely distracted her from her work. She didn't tell anyone what was going on and tried her best to stay on top of her projects, but things got away from her, and she let a few people down, John among them. When her life settled down, she offered apologies, but the memory of her erratic behavior lingered on. John accused her of not caring about her work. Joan protested, "I do so!" John told Joan, straight out, what he required to believe her. "Let me see you follow through once in a while, and I'll believe you care." Joan, realizing that the better choice wasn't to defend herself, but instead to find out what John was missing, replied, "So you need to see me follow through once in a while? Fair enough. Tell me how often, so I know what you need from me to change your mind." John said, "How about for the next month, you come in on time and you don't leave until you're done?" And Joan said, "Done! Start counting the days, because you can count on me to be on time and stay until I'm done."

From that point on, Joan just needed to make sure that John was aware of her arriving on time and leaving when she was done. At the end of the month, she pointed it out to him. "John, you said you would change your mind if you saw some things. Well, you've seen them. Are we good now?" And John says, "Joan, I'm impressed. It's good to know I can count on you." *Click*.

5 Ways to Manage Trouble with Gossip

If someone is gossiping about you, it can interfere with your ability to click not only with the source, but also with others who are subjected to the gossip. To manage the damage, you'll need to stop the behavior and build the connection. You will create an opportunity to develop the relationship at the same time you are nipping the problem in the bud.

1. Ask your source for details.

When someone comes to you and tells you that someone else is talking negatively about you, find out as much as you can. The more you know about who is talking this way and what's being said, the better able you will be to deal with it. Vague claims tell you nothing except how people feel.

2. Ask the gossip if it's true she has been talking about you.

If you trust your source, go directly to the person who is talking about you—or who you've heard is talking about you—for a face-to-face discussion. "I heard that you've been saying such and such about me. Is that true?" Gossip is a covert behavior and it only works when hidden away. You're not likely to get a confession, and you don't need one. But you will bring what was hidden at least partially into the light, and that will get the gossip's full attention on you and hand you an opportunity to change the dynamic in the relationship. Keep coming back and the gossip, uncomfortable with the light, will stop.

3. Don't let her change the subject.

"Who told you that?" is a gossip's usual response after having been called out. Don't be sidetracked. Restate your original question.

"Actually, the question isn't who said it. The question is, is it true? Are you saying these things about me?"

Whether she is or not, she's likely to deny the accusation. But it doesn't matter. What matters is that you're showing up and calling out the potential problem instead of letting it fester and grow in darkness. If she denies it, thank her for her time and apologize for taking her time. But while you've got her attention . . .

4. Use the interaction to get to know each other better.

It's harder for someone to talk badly about you when you share some of yourself and show an interest in her.

5. Plan for next time.

Let him know that he can talk to you. Invite him to come tell you to your face the next time he has something he wants to say about you. Present it as the more honorable and coura-geous choice—and a reflection of the kind of person you know him to be.

Putting the kibosh on gossip leads to clicking—and click-ing decreases the chances of gossiping.

6 Ways to Defuse a Meddler

When someone is interfering in your personal business, you're not likely to have any interest in clicking with her. But what if you could stop her meddling and start clicking with her all at the same time?

1. Understand what makes her so hard to please.

Maybe she has unrealistic expectations for you, and when you don't meet her standard of perfection or performance, she feels compelled to jump in. Maybe she is trying to prevent you from repeating her mistakes. And maybe—usually in fact—she just has too much time on her hands. If you can suss out the moti-vations behind the meddling, you may be able to address them directly and stop the interference.

2. Don't tell him he is wrong.

You will only put him on the defensive and reinforce the urge to interfere.

3. Receive it as a gift.

When she meddles, instead of fighting it or trying to correct the behavior, appreciate the intent behind it. Yes, I know, it is easier to say than do. But here's the thing: Better that she should be concerned about you than to care less about you, right? If it was a gift, what would you say? You'd say, "Thank you for caring." And that's just the right tone to click with someone who is minding your business instead of her own.

4. Give him something to do.

If a person is determined to be involved in your work or personal life, why deny him the pleasure of what he so obviously wants? For all intents and purposes, you can put yourself in charge of his behavior instead of being at the mercy of it. Since he is already interfering, give him a specific job in which his interference is welcome. For example, tell him to watch out for problems, or assign him the task of monitoring progress, or have him attend to a specific detail. The idea is that if you can give him something to do, that one thing may distract him from everything else. He feels involved, and you gain the freedom to focus on and do the rest. *Click.*

5. Question your questioner.

It's hard to click with someone who is interrogating you, but there's an easy way to turn the tables and create a click. If you find that someone has been asking you too many questions, ask her questions about *her* questions. Ask what her questions mean to her. Ask where she is going with her questions, or what's behind them. By becoming fascinated and curious about someone's previously unwelcome curiosity, you can bring the behavior to a stop and replace it with a click.

6. Be prepared with the answer.

When something is predictable, you can plan for it. Have a response that allows you to successfully deflect the question without deflecting the questioner.

That's what Macile did when she was fed up with her aunt's constant nagging about when she was going to get married and settled down. The next time her aunt poked her nose in, Macile replied, "I'm waiting until I can find someone who loves me the way Uncle Rod loves you, and that I can love as much as you love Uncle Rod," knowing full well that her aunt wasn't all that happy with her hubby. Her aunt immediately changed her tune. "Listen honey," she said. "Don't rush into something that isn't right for you. Better you should be happy." That was the last time her aunt asked her about a marriage. From that point on, the question was, "Are you happy?" And Macile was happy. She didn't have to answer that other question any more, and she and her aunt had a new understanding to share. *Click.*

3 Ways to Handle Sarcasm

Sarcasm requires a quick wit. For the person who appreciates a quick wit, this can click just fine. For the person who fails to see the humor in it, however, it becomes the anti-click.

Some people use sarcasm when they think the people around them are taking themselves too seriously, but they may also be using the snark in their remarks to divert attention away from things they don't want taken seriously. Sarcasm can also be a way of taking a shot at someone, a way of mixing humor and hostility to devalue the opinion of others. In this form, it is an expression of aggression, and it may imply that the user is uncertain about what he or she thinks about you. If you dig out the actual meaning and take offense, or if what they imply turns out not to be true, they can say you took it the wrong way.

1. Have a laugh at your own expense.

If someone is teasing you, laugh with her. If she seems to be provoking you into an argument, say, "That's certainly one way of looking at it!" If she makes fun of something you did, say, "Yeah, I guess it *is* kinda funny." When the humor is harmless, treating it that way gets you the click. And if the humor isn't harmless, it deflates the attempt to cause harm.

2. Take it at face value.

Turn the sarcasm around by taking it at face value. Typically, the person who uses sarcasm will detect a responsive sarcasm in this literal interpretation of his remarks. He says, "I wish I could lower my IQ so we could have a meaningful conversation." And you say, "Me too. That's got to be hard for you." Resonance through blending. *Click.*

3. Playfully put it back on her.

Sometimes the best defense is a good offense. If you know it's coming, giving as good as you get can give you the best click yet.

This may mean working on your material ahead of time. The simplest approach is to look at the sarcastic person earnestly and ask "Really?" to whatever she says about you. And then wait for her to answer. Repeat your "Really?" refrain every time she says something sarcastic.

Years ago, one of my clients, a hairdresser, offered me free haircuts for life. Anytime I showed up at her salon, she'd move me to the head of the line. I loved knowing that I could get a haircut quickly and easily, one permanent check on the "To Do" list of life.

Problem was, I never paid attention to the effect this arrangement had on all the people sitting in the salon patiently waiting their turn when I showed up. There was no click with them, that's for sure. Not that I noticed. Until the day when another employee there, Lucy, spoke up as I made my way to my client's chair: "Wow, it must be nice not to have to wait your turn like everyone else!" Now I noticed. And I wanted to turn it around.

I looked Lucy in the eye and said, "Really?"

"Yeah, I don't know who taught you your manners, but she should ask for a refund."

And I laughed. Then repeated, "Really?"

Then *she* laughed. Out came her last not-so-veiled attempt at indicting me for cutting in line. "You'd think your mother would have thought of that."

"Really?" I asked.

"Yes, really."

As I made my way to my friend's hair-cutting station, I said slowly and sarcastically, "Really!"

I became friends with Lucy from that day forward. She'd see me on the street and stop to talk. Or in the salon, she'd point the way. "Your chair awaits."

Click.

Dealing with the most troubling behaviors that interfere with clicking may take some practice on your part, a little mental rehearsal to get comfortable dealing with people in these ways. But when you do, no matter what the negative behavior interfering with a positive relationship, you'll find yourself clicking with people you never thought possible.

CHAPTER 9

The Click Zone

Clicking with Your Idea

Once someone gets you, the next level of clicking is to get him to get your good ideas.

Every human invention, every bit of progress, began as an idea. You've probably had a few good ideas of your own over the years that were misunderstood or tossed away. It's likely that the problem wasn't the idea, but the presentation of it. That's a shame, really, because you may have then drawn the conclusion that the idea wasn't so good after all. To get people to click with your ideas, you've got to learn how people receive information, and therefore how you should organize and present information to get it to them in the most advantageous way.

> You've got to learn how people receive information, so you can present it to them in the most advantageous way.

When you know how to get people to click with your ideas, your influence grows along with your impact—you matter to more people, and this gives you even more opportunities for click.

Let people play a part in developing your idea. Having others involved can lead to important refinements that will make your ideas more workable. And there is the added benefit that when people play a part, they have some ownership over its success. You don't have to follow every refinement someone else suggests—this is what critical thinking is for—but you should be open to discussion and exploration.

This Is a Test

Your mind tests all new input, whether it's an opinion, raw data, potentially relevant information, or an idea, by running it through a set of filters (your needs, motivations, and values). What you accept, what makes it through the filters, arrives at what I call "the click zone." From there, it can be used to inform, to transform, and to move you to action.

The better you understand what makes you tick, the stronger your understanding of how you pay attention, the more choices you have about what to do with incoming information, including how to present it to others.

Your ability to persuade someone, to get her to get your idea, depends on closely targeting what you say to get into the click zone right away. Have that intention the moment you begin to speak.

Open-Minded/Closed-Minded

The closer your idea matches with someone else's, the easier it will be for him to click with your idea. This does not mean that you have to completely share another person's point of view to connect, but it does mean that the person needs to recognize at least some of himself in what you say right from the outset.

If someone hasn't already made a big investment of time or thought or energy in your subject, or doesn't identify so strongly with it, or has not yet arrived at a conclusion about it, she is more likely to have a wide zone of acceptance. She will be more receptive and open-minded. It won't require as focused an effort to get her to click with your idea.

We witnessed this in the 2008 presidential election. Some people made up their minds early on and didn't budge over the umpteen months of campaigning: They were ready to cast their ballot long before election day rolled around, and pretty much nothing anyone could say would sway them. There was also a large block of uncommitted voters who were waiting for resonance. They sought a candidate who more closely shared their values, who better understood their needs. The candidate that could successfully fill those requirements for them would get their vote. Hard-core political junkies might have wondered how much more distinct the choices could possibly be. But one thing McCain and Obama had in common: They weren't trying to reach the voters who had already rejected them. They were aiming for those with the wider click zones, where they could actually get their ideas heard.

Dealing with Rejection

In the wake of rejection, the two most important things to remember are: *Stop.* And, *go back.*

You've obviously missed something fundamental, and until you recognize it, you'll not make progress in building the connection.

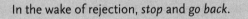

In the wake of rejection, *stop* and *go back.*

Take, for example, a waitress who got things off to a bad start with one table of diners. She was in a bad mood and her mood affected her customers' moods, and after a short while their behavior became, well, rude. Everything she said and did seemed to make things worse. And she became increasingly frustrated and confused by it.

Finally, she stopped trying to go forward. She actually unset the table, without saying a word, picking up the menus, water, silverware, place mats, everything. Then she came back to the table and, as she set down water for everyone, she said, "Guys, we're starting over. Hello! Welcome! My name is Denise, and I'm here to help you have a delicious meal and a pleasant afternoon. Can I bring you anything from the bar to get you started?"

The patrons laughed away the earlier difficulty, and by the end of the meal, Denise got a sizable tip. As she should have.

If you ever get off on the wrong foot with someone, if a conversation slowly or suddenly makes a turn for the worst, there's no call to keep going; back up and begin anew. Admit that you've gotten off on the wrong foot. Ask, "If it's okay with you, I'd like to start from the top, and this time, really give you my best."

Listening Tells You What to Say

The key to unlocking the click zone is to invite someone to talk, and then *listen*. The more certain a person is, the more precise and understanding you have to be. Notice the intensity in facial expression and vocal inflection, because the more intensely a person holds to an idea or position, the bigger the deal you must make of it. Speak to what you've learned, and you'll find your ability to introduce your ideas greatly enhanced. You don't have to hit a bull's-eye when you share ideas with people but you have to be familiar enough to make it into the click zone.

CHAPTER 10

Emotional Click Signals

WHEN IT COMES TO GETTING PEOPLE TO GET YOUR IDEAS, appealing to both logic and emotion is a surefire combination. What you say has to feel right before people will connect with it and accept it as right.

Most people like to think of themselves as logical, reasonable, and thoughtful. But feelings help us interpret facts. Emotions grab our attention and motivate us to focus on the issues in front of us. In the absence of emotion, humans turn out to be very bad at making decisions. This is demonstrated by the work of Dr. Antonio Damasio, head of neurology at the University of Iowa College of Medicine, who studies brain-damaged patients. (For more, you can check out his book, *Descartes' Error: Emotion, Reason, and the Human Brain.*)

You don't need clinical research to know for yourself the role emotions play in getting people to click with ideas. Just examine your own life. Some of the worst decisions you've ever made were based on feelings. And some of the best, too. Have you ever acted on impulse? Gone with your gut? Your ability to think is essential to navigate the complexities of modern life. But your emotional state also affects your ability to reason; sometimes your feelings are so strong, they override what you think completely.

Feelings *happen*, but thought requires *energy*. It takes a lot of energy to think. Literally. Here's the math: Thinking actually burns three times as many calories as not thinking. You burn one-tenth of a calorie per minute when your brain is doing nothing but stayin' alive, but that jumps up to one and a half calories per minute when you do a crossword puzzle. For comparison's sake, you burn four calories a minute while walking. According to some research, thinking really hard can create the same brainwave patterns as physical pain. No wonder we tend to avoid thinking when it isn't absolutely necessary. That makes us, according to psychologist Ellen Langer, "cognitive misers." We don't want to think unless we absolutely have to, even when people are talking to us.

Fortunately, we don't have to pick between logic and emotion in decision making. More often than not, humans use a combination of both. We decide emotionally and then justify the decision logically.

The 7 Signals

To make your ideas emotionally attractive and add persuasive power to the facts and logic of what you have to suggest, you can appeal to seven core signals that serve to capture the attention of others, helping you to click. They are:

- Affinity
- Comparison

- Conformity
- Reciprocity
- Authority
- Consistency
- Scarcity

Using the 7 Signals to Click

Receptors for these signals are hard-wired into our DNA, where they serve a valuable function in linking our society together and keeping those links intact. You are constantly on the receiving end of a variety of these signals from everyone you meet—almost always more than one at a time.

You are always broadcasting them yourself, too. Often these signals are sent unconsciously, out of a natural desire to connect. Knowing how to send the signals intentionally comes in handy when you want someone to click with your ideas.

You'll get the best effect when you combine signals. Not all signals work equally well in all situations. The more signals you can use, the stronger the idea is emotionally. And don't overdo it: A little signaling goes a long way.

Understanding the Signal of Affinity

When someone shows her appreciation, offers an opportunity, or gives us some much-needed attention—we know she likes us, and we generally return the favor. When we recognize that someone shares similar styles, motivations, and values, we're more receptive to what she has to say.

❏ **You click with people you find attractive.**

It may seem shallow, but people do judge books by their covers. Beauty may be in the eye of the beholder, and there sure is no accounting for taste, but if you find someone attractive, you'll feel some affinity with her. And it isn't always pretty and handsome that are attractive.

Bram makes jewelry and was selling his wares from a booth at a tattoo convention. For three days, he watched tattooed people coming and going and saw every imaginable combination of ink and metal on their skin. Halfway through the fourth day, a guy with metal spikes coming out of his bald skull, pins poking through his lips, big wooden dowels inserted in his earlobes, and tattoos across his chest, neck, and along his cheeks, stopped by the booth to look at a bracelet. Bram said, "I hope you don't mind, but there's something I'd love to ask you." In that moment, he sent the affinity signal, "I'm interested in you."

The guy said, "Sure, ask away!"

So Bram asked him, "Why do you have all this metal on your body, all this ink on your skin? What motivated you to do this to yourself?"

And the guy just laughed. He said, "Dude, to score with the chicks!"

Bram had a hard time making sense of that, until closing

time. That's when he saw the guy heading for the door, a tattooed girl on each arm.

He smiled broadly at Bram, gave a thumbs-up, and winked,
as if to say, "See what I mean?"

Taste may vary, whether it's Goth or hippy chic or the nerd
herd, or whatever floats someone's boat. But people click with
the ideas of people they find attractive.

❏ You click with charismatic people.

Some call it charm. Some call it suave. Whatever you call it, a
person who has this kind of clickability can walk into a room
and own it.

My mom used to tell me when I was a kid that "You get
more flies with honey than with vinegar." Charismatic, charming people are very persuasive.

❏ You click with those who treat you with respect.

When people seek to understand us and listen to us, when they
consider us as important as they consider themselves, we are
more easily persuaded to click with their ideas.

❏ You click with what people you like, like.

This is why companies choose celebrities to be spokespeople for
their products: When the public adores the celebrity, our affec-
tion for the celebrity rubs off on whatever product or idea the
company is trying to sell. We like yogurt Jamie Lee Curtis likes;
we like the charity Bono likes; we like whatever Oprah likes, and

that gives millions of her fans the idea that they want whatever Oprah wants them to have. By relying on the good judgment of people we like, much of our homework is already done for us.

This works even better with someone we personally know and like. We take reading recommendations from the members of our book club; kids want to wear the same brands as their best friends. If you're looking to date seriously, you ask your friends for introductions. Business people make hiring decisions based on recommendations from friends. We are predisposed to like our friends' friends.

Caveats About Affinity

It's great to be loved by others, but there are people who may use your desire to be liked against you, to leverage you into doing for them what you ought not do. Too much affinity may undermine your authority. Remember the rule: A little goes a long way.

5 Ways to Send the Signal of Affinity

1. Lead with your similarities.
You may well have your differences, but you should not dwell on those but rather focus on what you have in common.

2. Treat people with respect.
When people talk, seek to understand them, ask for their views, take them into account, and let them know they are important

to you. When you listen connectedly to people, you appeal to their better nature.

3. Let the other person know you like him.
Offer an honest compliment or your authentic appreciation. As my mom taught me, there's always something you can appreciate about almost anyone. Maybe it's nothing more than "Thanks for being honest about how you feel." As long as you mean it, it'll go a long way, even in a difficult situation.

4. Be charming.
True charisma is not something you can fake, but anyone can be enthusiastic, energetic, warm, and welcoming. When you approach, be approachable in return. Emotions can be contagious, so the person who is upbeat, energetic, and fun can win over a room full of people by how she is more than by what she does.

5. Watch your eye contact.
Not everyone responds to it in the same way. Some people feel like you're staring at them. Some won't feel connected unless they can look you directly in the eye. Observe how the other person uses eye contact, and reciprocate in kind.

Understanding the Signal of Comparison

Comparison allows people to more quickly size up their experiences and determine relative worth. When comparing good to bad, it's obvious that good is better. When comparing great to good, good pales in comparison. When someone compares her idea to a lesser one, or his effort to a weaker one, the signal is sent that something more or better has been offered and is deserving of our attention. After all, who doesn't like new instead of old, improved instead of standard, and helpful instead of helpless? Comparison sends the signal that it's time to click.

❏ **You click with the better of two choices.**
We compare whenever we're given a choice. If you walk into a store, and you see two similar items on the shelf, you're going to choose the one on sale. Or the one that has the better features. Or the one that has the most durability.

We do the same thing with ideas and with each other. With so many people coming and going in our lives, we have to narrow the field of possible connections somehow, distinguishing one person from another even when we know nothing much about them. So we do it partly on the basis of how they compare to someone else. When we size people up, we compare them to people we already know. And then we choose whether or not to be open to them.

> When we size people up, we compare them
> to people we already know.

Maybe we choose the person who makes eye contact with us when the rest of the group is wrapped up in other things, or the person with the easier smile, or, sometimes, just the lesser of two evils. Compared to the guy droning on about car repairs, the one with the one-track mind about politics seems like the better choice for passing time at a dinner or party. But compared to the one with the encyclopedic knowledge of pop music, maybe the political one is someone to steer clear of. And compared to the person mixing drinks or offering food, well, who cares about politics, car repairs, or pop music!

❑ **You click with people who match your ideals about how people should be.**

It is easier to click with those who measure up. When you meet someone who matches your preconceived notions, you are predisposed to click with him.

A person who uses language we deem inappropriate is not going to compare favorably with the person who speaks in the manner we deem appropriate. A person who dresses the way you expect a respectable person to dress will have more of your respect when he tells you his ideas. Following the negative press of President Clinton's Oval Office behavior, George W. Bush promised to restore dignity to the White House. He conveyed his respect for the office by making sure to always wear a tie in the Oval Office.

We also hold people to a standard of consistency, and are more receptive to their ideas when they are more the way we like them to be. It's easier to click with your grouchy boss the day he's in a good mood than when he's in a bad one, with your aloof teenager when she's doing something that really energizes her than when she's lazing around and being careless.

Caveats About Comparison

If your ideals are too lofty or too stringent, you're going to have a hard time finding anyone you deem click-worthy.

When you make too many comparisons, your comparisons lose their impact. Likewise, comparing one person to another person can undermine the power of your message. It sends the message that you prefer the others, and that's likely to lead to resentment and de-motivation. Pick and choose, the better to make the comparison between current performance and past or future performance. Like Olympic athletes, the best comparison you can make when it comes to performance is with yourself.

3 Ways to Click with the Signal of Comparison

1. Choose your benchmark carefully.

You need to look good by comparison. Whether the comparison is explicit or implicit, the question is always, "Compared to what?" Take care to set the standard to be sure you come out on top! (Without verging into braggadocio.)

2. Stand out from the crowd.

Draw that little bit of extra attention to yourself. The message you want to send is that you can fit in while standing out, rather than standing apart. Dress a little nicer, stand a little taller, walk and talk with more confidence. Articulate when you speak, smile, be considerate, be attentive to details. Volunteer to help, show your gratitude with a thank-you note, respect other people's time, or listen when everybody else is trying to talk. When everyone else is heading toward the door, stick around a few minutes to help clean up.

3. Compare yourself to yourself.
When you have a history with someone, you may want to reference yourself over time. Build on your strengths. Point out your personal improvements. Highlight your good mood ("I'm having a great day!") or your new openness ("Now you have my full attention!") or your change of heart ("I've come to realize that this is something very different than I thought it was.")— whatever will make you look better when compared to the version of you someone has encountered before.

Understanding the Signal of Conformity

You and your ideas are more likely to click with a group that perceives you as an insider rather than as an outsider. Numerous studies have shown that we are influenced by the groups of which we are a part. But it's not just people that conform to groups. Living creatures move collaboratively to fulfill common goals and move collectively against common foes. It is a passive defense mechanism that aims at quickly reducing as many differences with the group as possible so as not to be singled out for attack. Conformity has profound survival value, and it makes clicking with a group possible.

Cultures and communities are collections of people organized around areas of commonality and acting on those same instincts. Whether for food and shelter, security, or just belonging, it's usually better to stay together than to stand apart, to find a way to fit in rather than get too far out. Our ability to survive as a society, and thrive as individuals, depends on our ability to get together, work together, and move together toward our collective greater good. So if you want a group to click with your idea, that idea must contribute to the group's shared interest. If you want an individual to click with your idea, that idea must signal to the individual that it makes them part of a desirable group.

❑ **You click with ideas that belong to your community.**

We want to be part of something greater than ourselves. We join together to pursue the cause and be part of the movement, and we support the person who knows how to bring us together. This urge to merge into communities translates into companies that are famous as great places to work. Building that sensibility means creating signals of shared identity, from shirts to caps to departmental softball teams that want to wipe the field with the other departments.

The ways in which we conform speak to our sense of identity. Even nonconformists band together. Whether it's the nerds, the geeks, the beauties, the jocks, the "in" crowd, church groups, or political activists, birds of a feather flock together. It is in your interest to make note of these tendencies anytime you want people to connect with your ideas, so you can present your ideas as a way to fulfill those tendencies.

❏ You click with the ideas of the biggest crowd.

When we have the chance to follow a trend, we do. And some of those trends, in hindsight, are enough to make us blush now. From handlebar mustaches to Beatle wigs, from Walkmans to iPods, from big purses to tiny pooches, going with the crowd is built into us.

When a crowd gathers, it may not be any group we know, but if it's a growing group that's trending toward the same behavior, we eagerly rush to see what is going on, and thus grow the crowd and make it ever more attractive. "What's going on?" we ask. "We don't know!" comes the answer. But that doesn't stop us. If the crowd is there, something must be holding it together, even if it is nothing more than the shared experience of not knowing what's holding it together.

Get a crowd to gather around an idea, and the idea will attract and click with a bigger crowd.

❏ You click with whomever is popular.

Some people are simply more popular than others. When you look more closely, you'll see that those popular people are sending affinity signals *and* conformity signals. As more people recognize someone as popular, the larger the group around that person becomes, and the more people will want to join that group—thus, the more popular that person becomes. If we see a conference speaker with a big group clustered around her after her speech, we feel sure we can be a part of that connection when we approach. When the populist politician, the "man of the people," comes through town, the town turns out in droves. The more people come out, the more other people come out to join them. If you can represent your idea as popular with others, it is more likely to be received well than if it is presented as an unpopular idea, no matter how good it is.

Caveats About Conformity

People want to fit in, but not too tightly. Too much conformity can harm your chances of standing out. Too much conformity can compromise innovation and creativity. Use conformity where it counts, and leave the door open for the unexpected when conformity isn't absolutely necessary.

5 Ways to Send the Signal of Conformity

1. Help others be popular.

The more people you click with, the more people will click with you. Build a network of people around you by helping them build their networks inside of your network. Be inclusive, find your allies, and build a movement.

2. Join the community.

A community of shared interests, values, and goals is a great entry point for connection with individuals. Find their gathering place and gather with them. Find their interests and share in them. Communities are more about give than they are about get. To join a community, contribute to it.

3. Identify common goals.

Play up the ways you can work together and highlight a trend or movement or cause of which you are a part and in which the person you want to click with wants to be a part. Help the other person feel she is part of something larger than herself, even if that thing is just whatever is going on between the two of you at that moment.

4. Conform to the other person's expectations.

Be how he wants you to be, behave how he thinks you ought to behave. You can help set his expectations by pointing out how others in the same situation have dealt with it.

5. Point out how your idea fits their expectations.

Underline how your idea matches with their motivations and values. Make the connection between your idea and all that's gone before, so that it blends in rather than stands out too much. "The best in our industry have set something like this as the standard, so we'll be in great company if we do this."

Understanding the Signal of Reciprocity

Reciprocity is all about a little give and take. That's the old quid pro quo ("something for something," if you don't speak Latin) that you occasionally hear about. The instinct for reciprocity kicks in whenever we feel obligation. It's an effort by our nervous system to discharge that obligation as quickly as possible.

Whatever you do unto others, there's a very good chance that they will want to do unto you. What we do for one another evokes some degree of obligation. Helping one another helps us to build support systems on which we may come to depend.

❑ **You click with the ideas of people who do favors for you.**
We get a good feeling when someone places our interests equal to his own. Regardless of costs in terms of time, money, or energy, the favor speaks for itself, and the stage is set for a click. Even small favors will make you feel indebted (as well as grateful), and returning the favor can take the form of accepting the other person's ideas.

❑ **You click with people when you do favors for them.**
It's the other side of the coin. We feel good when we do for others, and we do good for others when we feel good about them too. The favors we do for others increase the possibility of them wanting to do favors for us, including the acceptance of our ideas.

❏ **You click with people who make sacrifices
   on your behalf.**

Whenever someone experiences a hardship in order to make our lives easier, that sense of obligation kicks in and amplifies the gratitude we feel for her service. The sacrifice of soldiers for our freedom moves us to support them and want to give them everything they need. The sacrifice of our parents invokes in us a sense of duty to them, which helps keep families together later in life as they experience the loss of independence that comes with age. And when the waiter in a restaurant or the salesman in a car dealership says, "Let me see what I can do for you," it's usually his way of invoking that same reciprocal sense of obligation that leads to bigger tips or closing the sale as the relationship arrives at its natural conclusion.

Caveats About Reciprocity

Don't be a doormat. Too much give can make you vulnerable. Constantly showering someone with favors helps no one. Make sure when you give of yourself to help someone out that you're receiving as well. Consistently performing favors with no reciprocity can make you look weak.

5 Ways to Send the Signal of Reciprocity

1. Look out for other people.

Be generous with others. Offer assistance and pitch in when the opportunity presents itself. Do someone a favor, or just offer to do someone a favor. Serving others, while rewarding in and of itself, also generates obligation to return the favor.

2. Let others do for you.

The fact is that sometimes the greatest gift we give others is receiving what they have to give. And anytime someone does something for you and you let her, she may feel more connected to you than before.

3. Go first.

Be the first to listen, the first to wait, the first to care, the first to share.

4. Highlight how your idea serves others.

Show that your idea is a favor to them. "This proposal is going to benefit the entire team, the company, and the community. That's why I put so much time into developing it. Because I can see what a difference it will make."

5. Let them know you're willing to sacrifice.

Indicate your willingness and ability to endure any hardship in order for your idea to succeed. "I want you to do this. So I'm going to bend over backward to make that happen."

Understanding the Signal of Authority

When you signal authority, other people will be inclined to click with you—and your ideas.

The ability to observe who is in power and then respond obediently is innate. Our nervous systems have evolutionary programming to keep us safe, and one powerful way to do this is to defer to the strongest, smartest, most capable, and most powerful among us. Acknowledging authority lets us know who to follow in a crisis or when facing uncertainty of less dire kinds.

We are designed to hear and obey, and our training enhances those natural tendencies. A system of authority is necessary for any community that wants to survive. All cultures reinforce obedience. Through conditioning that starts in childhood, just about everyone divides the world, consciously or not, into people we ought to obey, and people who ought to obey us.

Obedience to authority also can give us cover for our actions ("I was just following orders!"). In other words, it is yet another shortcut to deciding what to think or do (without spending too much energy thinking).

❏ **You click with the appearance of authority.**
If, at first glance, a person looks authoritative, this may cause us to grant her authority until we come to know her better. Authority can be signaled through manner of dress, social status, titles, and demeanor.

Uniforms are an obvious symbol of authority but we are also attuned to more subtle physical signs—self-confidence, ways of speaking, and the like. We are instinctively drawn to people who seem to know what they are doing. We notice when people seem to be in charge of themselves—they tend to invoke the same confidence in the people around them. We recognize people like that as someone we can trust, someone we can rely on—someone whose ideas matter.

❏ You click with the ideas of people who have more experience.

People assume that experience begets wisdom—and wisdom carries authority. You don't need a degree or a title to have the authority that comes from experience. But you do need experience! People need to have confidence that your experience is relevant. If the experience is real, it should be able to stand on its own as a credible source.

In my life, I've had the good fortune to meet many amazing individuals whose success had nothing to do with education or titles—but whose life experience qualified them to be of great service to others. Ray Kroc, for example, dropped out of high school at fifteen and went on to create the fast-food industry (McDonald's). Steve Jobs dropped out of college and founded one of the world's most successful technology companies, Apple, in a garage. Mary Kay Ash, after watching her manager promote less experienced and less qualified people past her simply because she was a woman, took fate into her own hands to found the highly successful Mary Kay Cosmetics. These people all excelled by turning their experience into authority. The stories of their backgrounds, combined with their gumption and drive, signaled to the people around them that they were people to be recognized, respected, and favored.

> Confidence in oneself and one's ideas
> grants the aura of authority.

Life is a hard teacher. She often gives the test first and the lesson after. But a person who learns from his experience grows in confidence. Confidence in oneself and one's ideas, garnered through life's challenges, grants the aura of authority, paving the way to a click.

Caveats About Authority

Too much authority can have the opposite effect of creating click, particularly with someone who has a tendency to rebel against it. Temper your authority with a few other signals and you are likely to be more successful.

Authority is so powerful, and obedience to authority so ingrained in us, that it must be deployed responsibly. At the extreme, blind obedience can lead to something like the Holocaust, where soldiers and civilians alike participated in atrocities simply because they were ordered to do so. The classic experiments conducted by Stanley Milgram delved more deeply into this phenomenon. In his research, volunteers gave electrical shocks to other volunteers at what they believed to be deadly levels and in spite of screams of protest, simply because someone in authority told them to do so.

7 Ways to Send the Signal of Authority

1. Carry yourself with authority.

Confidence is found first in your posture. When you stand tall, with your shoulders relaxed, instead of rounded and shrinking into a smaller physical space, you project a degree of self-assurance. When you introduce yourself instead of waiting to be introduced, you appear confident. While the occasional self-deprecating remark makes a confident person more accessible, too much self-doubt undermines others' ability to believe you. Observe people that you recognize as confident—as having authority—and model the way they carry themselves. As a person with authority, you don't need approval or agreement to believe in yourself. Before you walk into a room, remind yourself, "I'm the right person, in the right place, at the right time."

2. Speak from experience.

Rather than making assertions and statements about "how it is," the authoritative person speaks from his experience. Simply starting a sentence with the phrase "In my experience . . ." will alert listeners and invite them to pay closer attention.

3. Dress for success.

Always try to dress slightly better than the person you want to click with your idea, and be understated in your accessories and fragrance. Neat and clean clothing makes a stronger impression than dissonant and dirty duds. Casual clothing looks great, but not if you look like a slob while wearing it. There are regional differences in how people dress professionally, so look around and notice people that you see as successful in the environment you're stepping into. What are they wearing? Dress yourself accordingly.

4. Emphasize your credentials.

If you choose to represent yourself as an authority, make sure you can back it up. If your authority isn't authentic, it will be worthless once someone gets to know you. Cite your specific experiences, invoke your track record, and provide references.

5. Accept responsibility.

People sometimes prefer that others be in charge because it gives them cover in case something goes wrong. Exercise your authority by letting the other person know you're willing to take charge and take the blame.

6. Invoke other authorities.

In some cases, the authority of others is even more compelling than your own. Enlist other authorities to either bolster your case or to carry the case for you. If someone can speak for you, make the first contact for you, or provide a reference for you, you'll find it makes it easier to click. My parents were pros at this: When I was at the age when I simply could not be seen as giving any credence to anything Dad had to say, my father enlisted my favorite uncle to talk sense to me as the occasion required. For her whole life, my mom clipped things out of magazines, highlighted key messages therein, and mailed them to me, as if to say, "Don't take my word for it—take theirs!"

7. Be the authority.
Be self-controlled rather than controlling of others. Be credible and evenhanded. Be the authority you want to see in the world.

Understanding the Signal of Consistency

We want things to work the same way tomorrow that they worked yesterday. Consistency helps us to make sense of the world in which we live and to understand how we fit into it. We fully expect consistency in the behavior of others. If we can assume someone will act the same way, hold the same values, and follow the same rules as she did the last time we interacted with her, we save the time and effort of having to relearn all those things about her every time we meet.

Inconsistency creates a cognitive dissonance, a state in which our expectations are not met, and the world, at least for a moment, does not make sense. Our pulse quickens, our blood pressure goes up, and we get a bit sweaty. We become confused, our activity interrupted.

In a word, dissonance is uncomfortable, and often intensely so. When forced to confront inconsistency, we try to discharge it as quickly as possible. We dismiss it by saying it doesn't matter, or explaining it away. Or we overwhelm it with counterexamples.

> Consistency helps create the trust at the
> foundation of any positive relationship.

Moreover, this desire for consistency explains the difficulty people have changing their minds, admitting when they're wrong, or finding a new way to do something. It is in our natures to want to be consistent in the things we think, feel, and do. Psychologists call it "cognitive consistency." Our desire for consistency is so strong that we associate it with personal strength and character. Conversely, inconsistent behavior makes us feel like we can't trust someone. Consistency helps create the trust at the foundation of any positive relationship, laying the groundwork for a click.

❏ **You click with people when you know you can count on them.**

If a person makes a promise and delivers on that promise, we come to count on him. In a world in which there are so many moving parts and changing variables, there is great relief in being able to count on anyone or anything. Trust opens the door for persuasive communication. If I know I can count on you, then your ideas must be reliable too.

❏ **You click with people when you fulfill their positive expectations.**

People rise or fall to the level of our expectations. In a conflicted and often disappointing world, most people want experience consistent with their expectations. When we fulfill their positive expectations, it feels like a promise kept. It's even possible to get someone to change their behavior by consistently projecting that it will change.

Tom used to come home from work angry and explosive. He'd walk in the door, and launch into an angry rant about his boss, his coworkers, and anything else that upset him that day. He seemed oblivious to the impact this was having on his family. His wife, Mary, grew tired of this consistently negative behavior. So she developed the habit of greeting Tom's rant each evening with these words: "Tom, that's not like you. I know you to be a loving and reasonable man, and when you walk through that door, you know I love you more than anything, and I think you love me more than anything too. So that's how I expect you to talk to me."

The first few times Mary did this, Tom felt ashamed of his own behavior. The cognitive dissonance between what she said and how he was behaving when she said it was intensely uncomfortable. But it didn't take that long for Tom's behavior to begin to match her projection. At first, he'd reply angrily, "Yes, I know." But soon, knowing what she was going to say, Tom began adjusting for it before opening the door. Twenty-one days from the time she began her new behavior, Tom had a handle on his own behavior. Now he walked through the door aware of his own behavior, and that made it easier for him to measure up to her positive projection.

Click.

❏ **You click with someone that you expect to click with.**

Having a history of positive connection with someone doesn't guarantee you'll have a positive connection every time. But it does give you leverage. The more consistently positive the connection, the more likely it is to stay that way. This is one of the keys to great friendships and great customer service. The more consistently positive the experience a person has, the more the person comes to expect a positive experience. After a while, the most negative experience gets explained away ("They're just having a bad day").

Reputations precede us. If word gets out that you're someone who is easy to get along with, people who've heard the word will measure you by it. This creates leverage for referral business.

Caveats About Consistency

Clinging to consistency for its own sake rubs people the wrong way. We say that such people are stiffs—they are rigid or inflexible. Be consistent in your expectations of others, in your principles, and in the standards you apply to others, but retain some flexibility and be resourceful.

3 Ways to Send the Signal of Consistency

1. Treat people in a consistent way.

You want them to know what to expect from you. Be someone you can count on, so others will know they can count on you.

That means that if you say it, you do it, not just some of the time, but every time. So make sure you can do it before you say you will. If something gets in the way and you are unable to do what you said you'd do, let people know as soon as possible. Keep their expectations in check and make sure you can deliver.

2. Be consistent in who you are, what you stand for, and what you value.

Be true to your word. Match your words and your deeds, your habits and your values. Keep your promises.

3. Point out consistency.

When you share your ideas, point out how they are consistent with the motivations and values of the person you share them with. Point out how your ideas are consistent with statements made by the person you share them with. Point out how your ideas are consistent, and how doing anything else is inconsistent. "This idea is a continuation of the process we began last May, and if we fail to follow through in this way, people who have been watching will be left wondering what happened to us."

Understanding the Signal of Scarcity

When something is rare, its value increases. As the tennis pro Andre Agassi put it, "What makes something special is not just what you have to gain, but what you feel there is to lose."

The capacity for people to want and need seems limitless.

Meanwhile, we have only so much time, so much energy, so much attention, and so much opportunity. If you can't have everything, there have to be trade-offs. Economics has been defined as the study of human behavior when dealing with infinite needs and limited means. Well, there's an economics of relationships, too. Scarcity plays a powerful role in human relationships.

If you have the thing that other people want, you appear to have some degree of control of your environment. And that draws people to you.

It's important to remember that scarcity isn't just about tangible things; it can apply to intangibles like time, information, appreciation, and honesty.

When we consider time with someone to be hard to come by, we desire it more and go to greater lengths to experience it. Isn't that the basis of so many one-night stands? Men and women go to great lengths in pursuit of one another, and the harder it is to get the guy or girl, the more desirable he or she becomes.

When we perceive information as rare or hard to get, as in privileged information, we consider it more precious and we desire it. That's why so much connection happens around gossip and rumor. It's also what makes compliments or praise much more powerful when they are doled out sparingly.

When we consider a business relationship more valuable than others, we are motivated to find a way to make that relationship happen. That's how so many people wind up in bad business deals: They don't want to lose an opportunity or let the deal get away. Scarcity is a potent signal, because real value is often hard to find.

❏ **You click when people make you feel special.**

Some people have a knack for making others feel special. It's in their eyes—in a crowded room, they look at you as if there is no one else around. It's in their manner—they can turn their back on the world just to face you. And it's in their words—speaking to you as if they know you better than you know yourself.

Some people have a knack for doing the opposite.

I was boarding an airplane. The line was long, but I was at the head of it, so I had the displeasure of hearing the one flight attendant give a heads-up to the other flight attendant when she looked up and noticed us coming: "Here come the cattle." Nobody wants to be treated like "another one." I wasn't at all happy about this and I said so. "It's not a herd, I'm not a cow, and that attitude is full of bull." She smiled and tossed me an extra bag of pretzels. I calmed right down. It wasn't the greatest click in the world, but it was better than nothing!

Whether it's special attention, special appreciation, or a special invitation, when you get the impression that what you're getting is the rare treat or special treatment, you click. When you feel valued above the ordinary, or are treated as one-of-a-kind, you can't help but respond. This same signal is in use when people play hard-to-get, but it plays out differently. When a person acts like she is special and requires special treatment from others, there better be an obvious and discernible sense of why she deserves that treatment (like, she's the Queen of England, or some other celebrity), or the response she is likely to get from others is rejection.

"Special" works as a giving signal, but rarely works as a taking signal. If someone treats you like you're special, it is compelling. If someone requires that you treat him like he is special, it can be repulsive, or at best, off-putting. So if you want to be treated as "special," you should practice giving special treatment to others.

❏ **You click when the moment is fleeting.**

Twice a year, I teach a communication class for medical students at the Southwest College of Naturopathic Medicine and Health Sciences. I enjoy teaching this class so much that I asked the president of the college if I might do even more teaching at the school. His response: "Right now, the students think of you as caviar. If you were here more often, they might consider you chopped liver."

> Reserve sharing your ideas, and when you do,
> people may take notice.

Real opportunity seems to come with a narrow window of time. Don't wait too long to embrace it. When the president of the company has a rare meeting with employees, they are likely to find it more valuable than if the meetings happen too often, or are too easy to arrange. When you call to ask for a meeting and find it difficult to set it up, when the meeting comes, you are more likely to make the most of it.

This is the missed opportunity for people with too many ideas. When the opportunity to hear an idea is common, the idea is devalued before it's even been heard. Reserve sharing your ideas, and when you do, people may take notice. I advise clients who attend meetings to be reserved, to keep from speaking up as often as possible. That way, on the rare occasions when they do speak up, people will sit up and take notice. By keeping the opportunity scarce, the value is increased.

The key words for this signal are *exclusive, limited opportunity,* and *one-time-only,* because they each send the message that now is the time to click with the idea!

Caveats About Scarcity

Being spare in your giving of approval and attention can have the opposite effect on people who need it in abundance. For one thing, roles can be reversed quickly. If you are stingy in giving approval, the people you're not giving it to may be stingy in giving it back. Create some scarcity by choosing time and place rather than amount, so it stands out when you do it and gives you an advantage.

5 Ways to Send the Signal of Scarcity

1. Keep confidences.

When people confide in you, put what they tell you in a vault inside of you.

2. Speak in confidence.

When you give people privileged access—"Between you and me . . ."—it tells them that what you have to say is valuable and that you consider them special enough to hear it.

3. Create a sense of exclusivity.

Not necessarily for the relationship as a whole, although that's one way to go about it, but offer up what is obviously not widely available. "You're the only person I've said this to." Offer a little of your time if you're chronically overscheduled. "I'll make time for you but the best I can do is five minutes." Offer your advice if you are generally close-lipped. "I don't like to give advice, but here's what I think you should do." Offer your innermost thoughts. "Can I tell you something I've not told anyone? I'm worried too!" Share yourself. Reveal parts of yourself you don't wear on your sleeve. "You probably would never figure this out about me, but I'm . . ." Create intimacy—by definition, available only in limited quantities.

4. Embody qualities in short supply in today's world.

The scarcity of qualities like integrity, loyalty, and honesty gives you added value and credibility.

5. Offer something not easy to get.

This can be tangible or intangible, a special price or an early look at something—as long as it is something of value. I'm not necessarily talking about bribery here, though you'd probably get some connection that way. I'm talking about being part of an exclusive group, or having access to limited information, or private access to key components of your idea.

What Signaling Can Do for You

With these seven signals, everyone can get people to click with them—and their ideas. The signals capture others' attention, make your ideas emotionally attractive, and add persuasive power to the facts of the situation, providing shortcuts that make it easy for people to tell that your ideas are the ones with which they want to click.

THE SEVEN SIGNALS OF CLICK

AFFINITY

- ❏ You click with people you find attractive.
- ❏ You click with charismatic people.
- ❏ You click with those who treat you with respect.
- ❏ You click with what people you like, like.

5 WAYS TO SEND THE SIGNAL OF AFFINITY

1. Lead with your similarities.
2. Treat people with respect.
3. Let the other person know you like him.
4. Be charming.
5. Watch your eye contact.

COMPARISON

- ❏ You click with the better of two choices.
- ❏ You click with people who match your ideals about how people should be.

3 WAYS TO SEND THE SIGNAL OF COMPARISON

1. Choose your benchmark carefully.
2. Stand out from the crowd.
3. Compare yourself to yourself.

CONFORMITY

- ❏ You click with ideas that belong to your community.
- ❏ You click with the ideas of the biggest crowd.
- ❏ You click with whoever is popular.

5 Ways to Send the Signal of Conformity

1. Help others be popular.

2. Join the community.

3. Identify common goals.

4. Conform to the other person's expectations.

5. Point out how your idea fits their expectations.

Reciprocity

❑ You click with the ideas of people who do favors for you.

❑ You click with people when you do favors for them.

❑ You click with people who make sacrifices on your behalf.

5 Ways to Send the Signal of Reciprocity

1. Look out for other people.

2. Let others do for you.

3. Go first.

4. Highlight how your ideas serve others.

5. Let them know you're willing to sacrifice.

Authority

❑ You click with people with the appearance of authority.

❑ You click with the ideas of people who have more experience.

7 Ways to Send the Signal of Authority

1. Carry yourself with authority.

2. Speak from experience.

3. Dress for success.

4. Emphasize your credentials.

5. Accept responsibility.

6. Invoke other authorities.

7. Be the authority.

CONSISTENCY

- ❏ You click with people when you know you can count on them.
- ❏ You click with people when you fulfill their positive expectations.
- ❏ You click with someone that you expect to click with.

3 WAYS TO SEND THE SIGNAL OF CONSISTENCY

1. Treat people in a consistent way.

2. Be consistent in who you are, what you stand for, and what you value.

3. Point out consistency.

SCARCITY

- ❏ You click when people make you feel special.
- ❏ You click when the moment is fleeting.

5 WAYS TO SEND THE SIGNAL OF SCARCITY

1. Keep confidences.

2. Speak in confidence.

3. Create a sense of exclusivity.

4. Embody qualities in short supply in today's world.

5. Offer something not easy to get.

CHAPTER 11

Make Your Point

ONCE YOU'VE MADE THE INITIAL CLICK, YOU HAVE A GREEN light to share your ideas. To do that successfully—to continue the click—you need to know how to share an idea and how to convey it persuasively. The key is to get other people to think of your idea as, at least in part, their own. To get there, you need just a few tools for clear and concise communication.

Keep It Short and Simple

During the exchange of ideas, you accomplish more by saying less. Franklin Roosevelt may have said it best: "Be sincere. Be brief. Be seated." How often do you find yourself listening to too many words that are actually saying too little? The more you hear, the less you probably care.

Practice delivering your message in the fewest number of words possible while still aiming precisely at your desired result. Here's how:

1. Put the most important information up front.
Like a journalist, you should lead with the main point. Take as little time as possible to introduce an idea. In describing this

book, for example, "It's about making connections," works better than, "Business books are more popular than ever in this down economy, and I realized I had more to say than my other books cover, but you wouldn't believe how many versions it took before I came up with the right way to talk about how people connect . . ."

2. Be specific.

Even though you are aiming to keep it concise, *do not* leave out important details such as names, places, and actions, or it will be difficult for people to follow you.

3. Don't tell them everything.

At least not at first. Give the bottom line clearly and early on. If the other person wants more information, she can ask for it. And if she doesn't need it, you won't bog her down with it.

4. Focus on goals, not process.

If there's an action you want someone to take, tell him the specific desired result rather than elaborating on the process of getting there. You can hash that out later, after you are already clicking.

5. Choose familiar words.

Use familiar words to make it easy for people to connect with your idea. You shouldn't be looking to impress anyone with your vocabulary. Use the words that express your thought most clearly and directly.

In the sections that follow, I'll suggest more ways to organize what you say to drive the results you want. They all work best when your first step has been to whittle away everything extraneous to get to the heart of the matter quickly and clearly.

Make Your Point, Make It Clear

Make your point obvious from the start. Give listeners a reason to pay attention. Be as direct as possible. Tell people what you're going to tell them, and why. Because when you talk to people, the last thing you want them thinking about is, "Why are you telling me this?"

(Make sure before you begin that your main idea is clear to *you*.)

Say something along the lines of: "I have a proposal that we *xyz*, and I think it will excite you as much as it does me. I bring it forward now because we have a unique opportunity that won't last long. Bear with me as I give you some of the key details."

Make Your Case with Examples, and Back It with Numbers

If you want your idea to click, you need to make it stick. Start with clear and interesting language, then pin it to the wall with a well-chosen example or story. A good example serves as a hook on which your listeners are going to hang everything else you say, which will help them remember what they've heard.

Statistics almost never count as vivid language or memorable examples. The problem is, statistics themselves have a low reputation when it comes to credibility. You can tell by the way we talk about them. "Figures lie while liars figure." "Statistics means never having to say you're certain." While statistics appeal to logic, they're not always logical. Eighty-seven percent of all statistics are made up. And I just made *that* up.

Use statistics sparingly.

This is not to say that you can't use statistics to strengthen a point. Numbers can support a point, they just can't make one. Use statistics sparingly and remember that a fact only makes sense when you put it in a meaningful context.

For example, Diane is raising money for the Southern Oregon Land Conservancy and regularly talks with potential donors about the importance of this cause. If you ask, she can tell you that, since 1978, the SOLC has conserved more than 8,100 acres of the region's working farms and ranches, river corridors, forests, and scenic lands. She could tell you that in the 5 years between 2000 and 2005, the amount of land protected by local and state land trusts using easements doubled to 6.2 million acres.

But she doesn't. Instead, Diane talks about people like David Atkin, who grew up on the banks of the Illinois River, bought his own farm there as an adult, and later worked with a group of friends and neighbors to create a land trust dedicated to the permanent ecological protection of the land he loved. "I wanted to make a place in the world for family farms. I wanted to safeguard the water supply. I wanted to contribute to the fight to slow global warming," he explains. "Most of all, I wanted my grandchildren to experience the beauty of this place." The numbers don't tell the story; David Atkin does.

When you do use numbers:

- Make the meaning as personal as possible. "The typical family of four will save $250 a year on their taxes" is usually more powerful than "The cuts trim x-billion dollars from the budget." Make numbers real, make them into examples, and vividly connect them to your audience.

- Give them meaning by turning them into familiar mental images. Instead of saying something is more than two hundred yards long, say it's longer than two footfall fields.

- Turn large numbers into smaller ones. Use *8 out of 10* rather than *80 percent*. And if it's *83 percent*, round it off to *8 out of 10* (unless precision is key).

Make Your Point, Then Point the Way Forward

Tell people what you want them to do. One thing I've learned from my work over the years is that people know exactly what they *don't* want. They know what they don't want to see, what they don't want to hear, what they don't want to say, what they don't want to feel, what they don't want to experience.

But if all you know is what you don't want, you don't know what you *do* want. Or how to get it. If all your actions are based on fighting against or withdrawing from what you don't want rather than aiming for what you do want—all you'll end up with is more of what you don't want.

When you want people to get your ideas and what to do with your ideas, simply tell them. Without direction, most people just keep trying to move away from what they don't want and wind up getting nowhere. So make your point, then point the way forward. The more specific you are about a desired direction, the easier it is for people to consider going in that direction.

> Focus attention on what to do and why to do it.

There are only three reasons why people don't adopt an idea: They don't know what to do, they don't know why to do it, or they don't know how to do it. So tell them what they need to know! Focus attention on what to do and why to do it—if people want to know how, they'll probably ask.

Just remember, providing direction is not the same as describing the path.

Repeat. Restate.

Repetition is no substitute for conviction. As poet Ralph Waldo Emerson put it, "That which we do not believe, we cannot adequately say; even though we may repeat the words ever so often." But when you have confidence in your idea, repetition can help you get your ideas to click.

> When you have confidence in your idea,
> repetition can help you get your ideas to click.

You can't just say the same exact thing the same way over and over, however. Say the same thing *in a new way*. Our brains crave novelty—but also reinforcement. When you repeat an idea using different words, it gives people the idea that they are hearing something new, while underlining what they've already heard. It's like that motto at Crazy Larry's Diner: "Our food is tasty, yet delicious!"

In the advertising business this is called "building response potential." It is supposed to take upward of seven exposures to an idea before a person really internalizes it.

Still, a little goes a long way. Too much repetition yields frustration and aggravation. You don't want to become the kid in the backseat asking "Are we there yet? . . . Are we there yet? . . . Are we there yet?"

There is an infinite number of ways to say the same thing differently, but here are a few of the easiest and best strategies for reiterating without sounding repetitious:

- Use different words to get at the same idea. If necessary, consult your friendly neighborhood thesaurus for ideas.

- Change the frame of reference. If you've already talked about how your idea applies to others generally, talk about how it applies to someone specifically—or how it applies to *you*. Or shift from talking about your idea in relation to the future to talking about past experience. Talk about it in terms of how you use it at work if you've been discussing how you use it at home, and vice versa.

- Back up your point with an example. This is a way of restating without monotony.

Remember, a little goes a long way. Saying the same thing two or three different ways will make your point stronger. Going on and on about it undermines the message.

The Rule of Three

It's been said that the third time is the charm. The rule of three is one of the most powerful, potent, and practical rhetorical devices ever devised. It is also one of the simplest.

A pattern of threes is generally more memorable. Whether introducing, delivering, or summarizing an idea, you'll make it more memorable when you use the Rule of Three to establish and complete a pattern.

Whether this is three points on a list, three phrases in one sentence, or three sentences building to a point, the same three steps apply: first, establish a reference point for your idea; second, reinforce the reference point; and finally, slide your idea right into the slot you've created for it. In this way, you build up an expectation and then satisfy it, embedding your idea into the thinking of the person you are talking to. For example, you want to suggest to a colleague that she should consider a new way to grow her company: "You want to build your brand." (*step 1*) "That means letting more people know about what you do." (*step 2*) "Have you ever considered hosting your own radio show?" (*step 3*)

Rhetorical Questions

Raising questions and then planting the answers in the minds of your listeners can make an opinion sound much more like established fact. It tilts the playing field toward consensus. And the ask-and-answer format saves your listener a little thinking, always a good way to set the stage for a click.

Make an opinion sound more like established fact.

For example, you want to share your feelings on a colleague's proposal. You could say it straight out and leave the floor open for discussion: "I think his proposal is a good one." Or you could set yourself up for the agreement of everyone else in the room: "Is Joe's proposal the best one for our situation? Clearly it is."

For an even stronger click, combine rhetorical questions with the Rule of Three. Ask three rhetorical questions, all requiring the same answer. "Has Joe done his due diligence? Yes, and it is obvious. Has he proposed something workable? Yes, he certainly has. Now, is it time to stop talking about it and get to work on it?" Pause. The next thing you say is, "Yes, it is"—but that third yes will appear in the mind of your listener *before* you say it because of the pattern you've set. When you do say it, you are confirming an idea he already has in mind.

Be warned, however, that rhetorical questions can also be used to put people on the defensive, which leads to no clicking at all. That's when a person makes a statement in the form of a question that implies or says outright something negative about a person. Statements like "Where do you think you're going?" and "You have a problem with that?" and "How many times do I have to tell you this?" are off-putting because of their tone and loaded language.

In summary, are rhetorical questions useful? Yes. Should you use them only on occasion for the most powerful effect? Yes. Should you be careful about how you use them, so that people click with you and your ideas? Absolutely.

Do More with Less

By taking what you know about a person's needs, motivations, and values, then packaging your ideas using the signals and these guides, you can deliver your ideas for maximum persuasive click. As always, you don't want to go overboard in applying any of these tools. Use them to enhance your interactions, not direct them entirely. Think of them as seasoning, not the main course. Too much, and you'll overwhelm the other person. Too little, and you'll dilute their power. Get it just right, and whatever you're serving will be at its most palatable and easy to digest.

CHAPTER 12

Stumbling Blocks

AS LONG AS YOU ARE SPEAKING TO A PERSON'S NEEDS, MO-
tivations, or values, you can expect to get a satisfying click with
your ideas; yet despite all you've learned and applied, and no
matter how well organized you are in your presentation, occasionally you are unable to get your idea across. There's something in the way: a stumbling block.

Stumbling blocks occur when someone's mindset makes it
hard for him to accept, implement, or change his thinking.
This can take several forms—confusion, inhibition, blaming,
and arrogance among them—which we'll look at one by one
throughout this chapter.

Getting people to click with your ideas isn't about convincing
them. It's about helping them convince themselves.

Only people can change their own minds. You can't change
their minds for them. You can, however, give them a moment
of self-reflection, a chance to hear themselves talk, and in many
cases, to hear themselves think. In other words, you can set the

stage for them to change their own minds. Getting people to click with your ideas isn't about convincing them. It's about helping them convince themselves.

Keep in mind that it might be the other person setting up the roadblock—but it might be coming from you. So make sure you've cleared your own path before you start clearing someone else's.

The Right Questions

When the time comes to go forward, no matter which stumbling block you've hit, your most powerful tool is a simple question. Questions can get you past all the various barriers and back on the road to click.

You do have to choose the right questions. To do that, you have to identify which roadblock you've hit. So the descriptions of each of the blocks that follow include information on how to know what you've run into. You'll also learn the specific lines of questioning that are most effective for each particular block. But generally speaking, you can use questions to get a derailed conversation back on track, lead people in the direction you want them to go, gather more information, solicit agreement, invite thought, or spur an emotional reaction. The way to know for sure what someone means by what she says is to ask her questions. The way to know what your idea means to someone else is to ask him questions after he's heard it.

Questions work better than statements when the road is blocked, because when you make a statement, people have only two options: agree with it or disagree. But a well-asked question will encourage people to think, regardless of whether or not they agree with you. And if they disagree with you, thinking about the answer to your question may bring them to something important they hadn't considered, increasing your chance of clicking.

Take Suresh's relationship with his manager, Matt, for example. When it seemed that all his suggestions about how to more smoothly run the design process met with nothing but resistance, Suresh used smart questions to turn things around. Instead of telling Matt his ideas straight out, he made the simple switch to running them by him as questions. He'd say, "Matt, I need your help with something. If I were to try doing it this way, what do you think would make it better?" Whatever the response, Suresh could build on it with more questions, as necessary, until either Suresh understood and accepted a *no*—or Matt gave the go-ahead. Without the constant clashing over ideas, the entire dynamic of their relationship changed for the better.

It's all about the questions.

It is possible to pile on too many questions, or ask them too quickly, which will make a person feel like she is being interrogated and give rise to more defenses rather than removing barriers. And here, too, you should always follow the guidelines about asking questions covered in earlier chapters, such as backtracking before asking a question, and being sure you get an actual answer to each question, even if it means repeating or restating the question.

Sometimes you may find that the questions you ask take you down the wrong road, instead of giving you access to an open road. If you should stumble while trying to remove a block, catch yourself, back up, backtrack, and try a different question.

Block One: Confusion

When confusion stands in the way of a click, either you or the person you are talking to is missing some information. Over-generalization, with key details missing, is the most common cause of confusion.

You can go a long way to avoid confusion by focusing on specifics. Steer clear especially of sweeping generalizations like *everything* and *nothing, everyone* and *no one,* and *always* and *never.* Watch out for the vague use of *they* or *them,* when exactly who you are talking about is unspecified ("They say those companies are in trouble . . ." *Who* says? *Which* companies?). Be as specific as you can and be sure to include the details the other person most needs to know (such as *who, what, where,* and *when*).

When you are confused about what someone is saying to you, ask for the missing information. Don't just start guessing and filling in what you *think* is missing! That's a recipe for more confusion. *Do* ask for what you need to know until you've filled in all the blanks. Ask specific questions that will get you specific answers. Ask until you are sure you understand the other person.

When people are most confused, they may barely realize it.

Asking your questions may help them get a handle on exactly what they mean to say, as well.

Once the confusion clears, your idea has a chance to click.

Block Two: Hitting an Impasse

One of two things creates an impasse: Either there's no plan in place, or someone reaches an undesirable decision. To get past this stumbling block, focus on how you got there and use that information to focus on how to move forward.

❏ **Find the road already taken.**
If someone has obviously already arrived at a decision or conclusion, you can ask how he got there. Listen for the thought process involved—you may be able to trigger that same process to help the person arrive at a different decision. Knowing how he thinks can help you tailor your approach and reach that click.

Consider Janelle, a VP of an insurance company, and Lillian, the head of marketing and client services, and their discussion about the best way to respond to the recent loss of their largest client in a shrinking business climate. Lillian thinks that the best response to a changing business environment is proactive rather than reactive—improve existing products and services for current clients and develop new products and services to attract new clients. When she tells Janelle her idea, Janelle declares that she's thought it through already and made up her mind about what to do. It's time to lay off some of Lillian's creative staff. Lillian thinks this is a terrible idea. After a brief back and forth, Lillian realizes that they are at an impasse. She knows arguing can't change Janelle's mind and may even harden her resolve, so Lillian decides to try a different approach:

"I get it. You've made up your mind. But please help me understand, since it affects my staff. How did you make up your mind?"

Janelle replies, "I looked at the numbers, talked to my advisors, and reached this painful decision."

Lillian backtracks what she's heard and then asks, "I'm curious, which numbers did you look at?" And when she has the answer, she asks, "Which advisors did you talk with?" And lastly, she asks, "How did you come to this decision based on those numbers and advisors?"

Each question has the potential to yield valuable information, while giving Janelle more information about her own thought process. Janelle might discover something she's failed to take into account.

And knowing Janelle's thought process for arriving at the decision, Lillian gains a new option for presenting her own idea. She can suggest that Janelle consider other numbers, like the amount the company has invested in developing the staff and the cost of losing any more dissatisfied clients. Finally, she can suggest that Janelle talk to other advisors who may have a different opinion. Then she can ask Janelle to revisit her decision.

Lillian's questions won't necessarily solve anything, but they may change everything.

❏ **Define a pathway forward.**

Ideas have a certain life cycle. First, the idea is born—someone thinks it up. At first, the idea may engage people. Momentum gathers. Excitement builds. And then . . .

. . . Nothing. Without specifics about how to go on, without plans for how to step forward, the idea grinds to a halt. Attention fades, neglect takes over, and eventually the idea just fades into history and is forgotten. Or the idea may just idle, not actually slipping away, but not proceeding, either.

You can prevent this ignominious end and give an idea a longer shelf life by setting out a way forward. And you can get a sidelined idea moving again by defining a way forward. Where no path is clear, ask questions about how to find it. Follow up your *who*, *what*, *where*, and *when* questions with one more: *How?* "How do we go forward from here?" And, if that's an unknown, then: "How can we find out?" Ask someone else, ask an expert, investigate it, and report back. Make a plan of action and act on it, one step at a time.

How questions can reveal the information that will help set new goals and point the way toward achieving them. They can reengage interest and motivation. Looking forward is the first step to moving forward. Tackling problems and making plans are, in and of themselves, ways of moving forward. A single step is movement. A series of steps is momentum.

Looking forward is the first step to moving forward.

Plotting a course ahead changed the game at XYZ Design Company. The employees there were never at a loss for ideas. One month, someone brought forward an idea for a wireless programmable toaster. The next month, a silent leaf-blower. These novel ideas got everyone excited, but then time would pass and inevitably they would fall by the wayside.

Production continued in a similar fashion until XYZ learned to plot the course ahead. How would programming the toaster work? How could they get it made in a cost-effective manner? How would the silencer on the leaf-blower work? How would they market it? The answers helped them rule out impractical ideas and bring the best ones to fruition. Responsibility was assigned, resources identified, and teams got their specific marching orders. I, for one, hope the silent leaf-blower is one of the ones that makes it off the drawing board!

Block Three: Getting Stuck

Ideas get stuck when they stop moving or when people lose perspective. Once an idea gets bogged down, the more you try to push it ahead, the more you'll be just spinning your wheels, and the more and more stuck you will get.

You can hear when an idea becomes stuck. The very words used to express it become passive and empty. Verbs become "frozen" into static nouns. We talk a lot about "customer service" or "business excellence" yet the concepts have become almost meaningless because they are divorced from the actions at their roots: to serve and to excel. Ideas get stuck when they become *things* instead of *processes* or *actions* in this way.

> Check the language you're using to make sure
> it is active, rather than passive.

To get an idea unstuck so that it can click, ask a question that contains the active form of the key word, to set things back in motion. Regain perspective by looking at the issue from a critical angle. Focus on action to get things going again. Check the language you're using to make sure it is active, rather than passive. If the company meeting on "customer service" seems to be going nowhere fast, for example, try asking, "How do we *serve* our customers? How *should* we serve our customers?"

Block Four: Inhibition

There are at least two ways to approach just about anything in life. You can either believe that anything is possible or you can believe in limitations. Since life is an exercise in self-fulfilling prophecy, when you believe that anything is possible, you are more likely to discover the possibilities. On the other hand, when a person believes that something can't be done, she will find evidence to support that belief. Perhaps you are familiar with the saying that "Whatever you can conceive and believe, you can achieve." The inhibited person has a different take. "Whatever I can't conceive, I believe." When people believe their options are limited, they won't be inspired to make the "impossible" possible.

Inhibition can be situational. A person who can see the possibilities of one idea may still find only limitation when considering another idea. Whether generally or specifically, an inhibited person holds back an idea by investing all her concern into identifying constraints and then placing them outside her control.

You can hear this, too, in his speech. Words like *can't*, and *have to, should,* and *must* litter his vocabulary. The choice of words binds and holds back ideas. People who have really bought into their limitations trade their creative instincts for such reactive reasons. They accept the limitation that they believe is in their way and assume it must be there for some reason. Finding out the reason for the limitation is the road less traveled. It's a road worth taking.

Dana works at a discount shoe store. One day, a customer named Suzanne asked for an advertised special but all the shoes of that sort were sold out. Suzanne asked, "Will you be getting more in?" Dana replied, "I don't know." Suzanne asked, "Can you find out?" And Dana said, with what sounded like great certainty, "No, I can't." Suzanne persisted. "What stops you from finding out?" Dana had to think about it. "I'm doing inventory." Suzanne offered an idea. "Can you find out first and then do the inventory?" And Dana replied, "Um, okay." Dana could have arrived at that conclusion sooner, only she was unable to see past the idea of her limitations. Suzanne, eager for the special, helped her by asking questions about what was in the way and then suggested a way by asking another question.

Inhibition can interfere with your relationships as well. This is what happens when you take an instant dislike to someone or make assumptions about someone based on limited knowledge. Maybe you figure your "blue state" self can't possibly connect with, or shouldn't connect with, the "red stater" you just met, or vice versa. Inhibited in this way, you won't even try. Or maybe you pass on the chance to chat with someone who knows just the person you're trying to meet, because you observe them engaged in a habit that you can't or won't tolerate.

How do you remove the stumbling block of inhibition? It won't do to argue with someone who believes in her limitations. Instead, find out how the limitations work. When someone says, "I can't," find out what stops her. When someone says she "should," find out what would happen if she didn't.

> Whether it's fear or doubt, find it out.

When an inhibited person is given the opportunity to hear her thoughts in the presence of a person who can see possibility, the stumbling block begins to fall away. Just the action of answering your questions may be enough to turn her attention in a new direction.

When people believe that a limitation is real, it inhibits them. To remove this stumbling block, your first task is to identify the inhibiting factors surrounding the acceptance of your ideas. Whether it's fear or doubt, find it out.

In Chapter 5, we covered fear as a motivator. If you know someone is inhibited by fear, one option is to frame your idea in terms of what she might fear about *not* adopting your idea.

Nan has a specialized piece of exercise equipment at her gym. It improves circulation by creating a jiggling movement throughout the body. One day, she invites her customer, Alice, to give it a try.

Alice looks at the equipment and then backs away from it. "No, I'm not interested."

Nan asked, "Not interested? In this *amazing* piece of equipment? Do you mind if I ask what about it are you not interested in?"

Alice said, "It looks like it would be uncomfortable."

Nan asked, "Really? Uncomfortable in what way?"

Alice responded, "Gosh, I would be embarrassed to use it. It would shake my fat and make me look ridiculous."

"I know what you mean about looking ridiculous, but what about shaking your fat would look ridiculous?"

Embarrassed, Alice admitted, "Well, anyone that walked in would see my fat rear end wiggling at high speed. What an awful sight!"

Nan thought for a moment. "That's interesting. You know what I would see? I'd see someone who was doing something to get in shape so she wouldn't look ridiculous."

And Alice, clicking with that idea, finally agreed. "Well, let me give it a try."

When you know what someone fears and how she thinks, then you can introduce a new possibility to her. Appealing to her train of thought and coaxing her away from her limitations will help her click with your idea.

Block Five: All or Nothing

In relationships, problem-solving, and especially creativity, all-or-nothing is a self-defeating mindset that will block a click every time.

There's nothing inherently wrong with thinking in extremes. There are times when this can help us see the big picture or put events in perspective, just as there are times when moving from the general to the specific is more helpful. When someone always and only operates in this mode, however, ignoring all the specific people, places, and things around her in favor of black-and-white thinking, it becomes all but impossible to click.

Fortunately, this is an easy stumbling block to identify and remove. When you're hearing words like *everyone, everything, always, never, nobody,* and *nothing,* you'll know you're up against all-or-nothing thinking. To break through the block, you need to ask the right questions that are designed to get a specific answer. If the talk is about "everybody" being there, find out who, exactly, attended; if it's about something that "always" happens, find out when, specifically, it occurs. You get the idea.

Once you have a specific example, offer a counter-example—someone who didn't go or a time it didn't happen—and the stumbling block will crumble.

❏ **Escalate with exaggeration.**

If basic questions and simple counter-examples aren't enough to loosen someone's grip on their black-and-white perspective, try exaggerating your question. If you really stretch it to the extremes, you'll shed light on the implausibility of her point of view and she may begin to open up.

Let's say Tom is reporting back about a presentation he's just given that you didn't attend. Tom wants to make a point about your absence and insists that everyone was there.

Call him out. Say, "Everyone was there? Every single person in the whole organization? Not one person called in sick that day, or totally forgot the meeting?"

Lest he be pegged as a liar, Tom will likely back down. "Well, not *every*one, of course, but let me tell you, it was standing room only while I gave the presentation and took questions."

This kind of exaggeration has to be applied with some degree of discretion and humor. If you come off as mocking or disapproving, your reaction will not be received well. So the use of exaggeration is an exercise in the subtle increase in voice tone and energy. Make sure the nonverbal cues you are sending indicate that you are on the other person's side and that these are just simple questions aimed at exploring what he's said.

❏ **Use the ultimate exaggeration: Agree.**

When a person thinking in all-or-none terms gets backed into a corner defending himself, he can become polarized against whatever it is you are saying. He's no longer thinking about what he's saying, he's just reflexively holding the line at everything and nothing.

This is the optimal time to deploy the ultimate weapon: Agree with him. Just tell him, "You're right." He won't expect you to agree so you'll have his undivided attention. Next, you should repeat and exaggerate his point.

A woman at one of my presentations stood up to declare that nothing I was saying would work. After some back and forth, I finally realized what I had to do. I told her, "Well, then, I guess you're right. It won't work." I paused. "Not for you, at least. No way, no how, not now, not ever. Not even you could find a way to make it work!"

At that point, she had nothing to say because I had said it all. She began to reply, but before she could argue with herself, I took the conversation in a different direction.

"I'm interested in what led you to this conclusion; please come talk to me at the end of the program." Then I continued on with my presentation as if we had reached complete agreement.

At the end of the day she approached me to apologize. Once she'd had time to think about it, her argument didn't make sense, even to her. She then asked for my advice on a completely different situation that was bothering her. My approach to dealing with her had opened up some room for possibility. That was all the space she needed for us to click.

Block Six: Blame

Blame is at the heart of many conflicts. It is so common that many times people don't even realize they are doing it. As long as someone is quick to blame someone or something else for whatever problem she faces, it is going to be difficult to click with her. It's all too easy to point a finger, turning yourself into a victim of circumstance rather than a creator of your own experience.

To move beyond blame and get to the click, you have to tease apart cause and effect. As I've explained before, the best way to get to the bottom of any problem is to ask questions. When the right questions help the other person recognize and accept that the cause of a problem is her own doing—that the resolution is within her control—you may be able to produce a click after all.

Imagine you're in the passenger seat of your friend's car. You happen to be a particularly nervous passenger and your friend is speeding around corners and zipping through traffic. Gripping your seat belt with eyes squeezed shut, you cry, "Slow down!"

Shocked by your outburst, your friend tries to defend herself. "That car was tailgating me, it's not my fault!"

You look behind, and there's no car for at least a quarter mile. No longer an agent of free will, it appears that your friend has ceded control of her accelerator to the driver of another car! You could yell that at her, which would only lead to more reckless driving. Or, if you actually want to get somewhere (in one piece, at that!), you could ask her, "How did being tailgated make you speed up?"

It may take some prodding, but eventually she'll get to the heart of the matter. It may not happen immediately, but asking questions will get you there. It doesn't require an especially self-aware person. The other person might not even know she knows the answer to what you are asking before you ask. But when you do ask, she will tell you. Through your questions, she becomes aware. So, your tailgating friend may admit, "I felt pressured."

Once she's able to put a name on the problem, the conversation can take a more productive turn and you can figure out—together—how to avoid that pesky tailgater and other pressures while driving. Instead of squabbling over whether she should have pulled into the other lane or kept going at a safe speed, etc., you and your friend avoid the roadblock and get back to clicking.

The blame game is a formula as old as time, but just asking about the immediate problem is usually enough for people to see what's really going on and deal with it accordingly. When you're trying to click with a person who's prone to laying blame elsewhere, there's no point in arguing with him. Instead, when someone is blocking your idea with blame, try asking her about the connection between cause and effect.

Let's look at a more business-related scenario. A few weeks ago, Cindy was asked to prepare a presentation with Janelle that unfortunately wasn't completed on time. Instead of taking responsibility for falling down on the job, Cindy insisted that her team would have made the deadline had it not been for Janelle.

Rather than argue with her, your best approach will be to ask Cindy, "How do you know you would have otherwise finished on time?"

Cindy will likely tell you, "It's obvious. Janelle finished late on the last project."

This is your opportunity to offer Cindy an alternate explanation for Janelle's poor time management. Ask Cindy a question that would require her to look at the situation in a different light.

"What differences were there between these two projects? What materials did she need and when did she get them?"

People may snap out of their blaming behavior as they begin to see the problem differently. More often than not, no matter how reasonable blame may sound, it is built of unfounded ideas that don't hold up to scrutiny. Asking the right questions can expose the circular logic, take blame out of the equation, and clear the way for a click.

That's what happened at Dan's Electronics when Julia figured out a new approach to discussing the store's slump with the owner. Dan had a million reasons why sales were spiraling downward—none of which had anything to do with him. Internet sales that were killing them, gas prices were too high, and, by the way, the economy was really lousy. "There's nothing we can do except pray for a miracle," he could often be found saying.

Always optimistic, Julia wanted to take a more active approach to improving the store and with it, her employment prospects. Since Dan was hooked on blaming external causes for his store's performance, Julia asked Dan straight out, "Help me make sense of this. How exactly has the slowing economy stopped customers from coming in?"

Quite matter-of-factly Dan replied, "Our products are luxury items. Nobody wants them."

"Who doesn't want them?" she persisted.

"Come on, Julia, face it. Most people have no use for these products."

Julia asked for a counter-example. "You say most people don't want our products, but something made you think starting this business was a good idea, right? So who *does* want them?"

Dan drew a blank. "Nobody," he repeated.

Julia made a point to exaggerate his response. "Nobody? Not one single person? Or family? Or group? Nobody at all?"

Dan chuckled. "Okay, well maybe somebody wants cameras and music players, but dang if I know who or where they are."

That gave Julia an idea. "Maybe that's the problem, Dan. We haven't identified who or where they are. What are we doing about that?"

Dan paused for a moment before he said, "Apparently not enough."

Julia had perfectly set up her introduction. "Maybe the economy will kill us, but we don't have to help it. I have some ideas for keeping this store alive."

She went on to suggest increasing inventory on lower-priced items to appeal to budget-minded consumers, running specials aimed at service groups and offering premiums to returning customers. Before too long, Dan was smiling and nodding his head. "You know, Julia, you're right. Let's get going on these and see which ones really work."

Click.

Block Seven: Excuses

Excuses *seem* to provide a credible reason to do or not do something, but in reality they serve to mask the *real* reason. To remove this stumbling block you need to help people find and express that real reason for avoiding a problem.

> Excuses serve mainly to mask the *real* reason.

We've all made excuses, but getting to the heart of the matter is another matter entirely. Your best bet will be to pointedly ask why the excuse at hand is a viable reason not to do something. Essentially, you want to create a situation in which the individual making excuses can look within and really understand what's giving her pause.

When you open the door to that moment of reflection, you open the door to *click.*

Consider the following.

Leopold had recently received an award from his company for developing an efficient message-delivery system. Due to the prestige of the award, he would have to travel out of state to the corporate headquarters to accept. Leopold's girlfriend, Nancy, while proud of his accomplishments, insisted that she wouldn't be able to go. "I have a deadline to meet," she told him one evening over dinner.

Crushed, Leopold couldn't see the problem. "How does having a deadline keep you from going?"

Nancy replied, "I'm so sorry, Leo, but I have only another three weeks, and your banquet falls right in the middle of that."

"I don't understand," he persisted. "How would traveling to the ceremony for one night make it harder to meet your deadline?"

"I wouldn't be able to get any work done while traveling," Nancy said.

Still not satisfied, Leopold nodded as though he understood, but he could not wipe the confusion from his face. "Help me understand this. How does travelling interfere with you getting any work done?"

So Nancy explained. "Well, when I travel, I like to kick back and relax, you know? Enjoy myself."

"I understand," he genuinely agreed. "Have you ever found that a day off gives you more focus when you get back to work?"

That's when Nancy realized that a little time away might be just what she needed to hit her deadline. She could take the trip, enjoy the dinner, and still get everything done. She just needed a little help to be able to see it that way.

Block Eight: Projection

When someone's premature opinions about you or your idea block that person's ability to actually learn anything about you or your idea, you've reached the projection block.

Projection occurs when a person takes some personal aspect, trait, quality, thought, or behavior and projects it onto another person. Often, the precursors to projection are misinformation and misconception. Shockingly, this is a normal human behavior, but it doesn't always have to be negative. Some forms of projection—like empathy and intuition—can actually lead the way to click.

You need to know a little something about a person before you can click with him—and he needs to know a little something about you. If the information he is operating with comes only from his projection, a click is impossible. And arguing with someone about what he *thinks* is true is pointless.

To avoid this block, you should always assume that unless someone *tells* you what she is thinking, you have no way of knowing. If you want to know what she is thinking, or if you want to challenge what she thinks of you, all you need to do is ask.

Galib sells training programs to help universities develop their online recruitment. When he discussed the service with Cheryl, an administrator for a university, she seemed interested in the product line, but declared it would never work in her department. "My division head, Tad, would never go for this."

Galib simply asked how she was so certain.

"He just doesn't go for this kind of thing," she replied.

"What kind of thing do you mean? How doesn't he go for it?"

Cheryl explained that Tad, hailing from a more traditional background, was not fond of change. "He's generally pretty closed-minded."

Galib nodded. "I've heard that before, believe me. How do you know Tad has a closed mind, though?"

"Last month, he shot me down when I suggested we try a new testing procedure," Cheryl replied with a shrug. "He's the kind of guy who's worn the same tie every day for years, Galib. We tried to buy him a new one for his birthday five years ago and it's still sitting in the box next to his desk. There's no point in even trying to convince him to use this software."

"I see," Galib said. "Do you think there's any chance he had something else going on that day besides considering your testing procedure?"

"Well now that you mention it," said Cheryl, beginning to think, "I might have been a little pushy."

"Ah! And how did that go over?" asked Galib.

"And I might have accused him of being resistant to change." Cheryl laughed. "Um, he didn't seem to care for it. In fact, I haven't talked to him about anything substantive since."

"Hm. Would you mind if I called him myself to talk about online recruitment? Or, if you prefer, we could call him together . . ."

Cheryl cut in before Galib could finish. "You know, I think I'll give him a call. I guess I owe him an apology. Then I'll see if he has time to see both of us. I think he'll love your product."

Click!

Block Nine: Arrogance

Arrogance is often a cover for weakness. A little investigation on your part will reveal that the underpinnings of someone's self-importance are faulty, a scaffolding of undeserved authority and unreasonable rules.

This is the penultimate stumbling block. People tend to place themselves at the center of their own universe and bolster that place with their own thoughts, needs, motivations, and values—unable to see others' wants, needs, and resources. Arrogance can also appear as a person with a seemingly very high opinion of himself talks down to you or belittles your idea to others.

The best way to confront arrogance is with confidence—either in yourself or your idea. Your conviction, however, should be based on strength, experience, and clarity rather than weakness, wishes, or blindness.

When faced with arrogance, don't defend your own ideas. The better approach is to ask the right questions to clear the way for click:

• **Ask for the source or a reference.** Just do it with tact. Start with a softening phrase, such as "I'd like to know," or "I'm curious," or "Can you tell me . . ." Try:

"I'm curious: According to whom?"

"Can you tell me how you know that?"

"Is that right? I'd like to know your source."

"Really? Do you know where that comes from?"

• **Ask what makes the source the most credible.** You can skip this bit if you've already heard a reliable source, like "this month's *Journal of Applied Biomedical Sciences.*" But if you don't think the source is credible (something like "my manicurist" or "the *National Enquirer*"), ask what makes that source the most credible one. If the other person resorts to hyperbole or ambiguity to describe her source ("Everybody knows . . ." or "It's obvious . . ." or "I heard it somewhere . . ."), simply repeat your request: "Still, I'm curious, where does that come from?"

• **Provide new information, sources, or reference points in the form of a question.** Don't *tell* them—run it by them, as if you desperately need their insight. "I'm curious to know what you think about something. Were you aware that . . . ?" or "That's really interesting. Did you know . . . ?" Running something by a seemingly arrogant person can change the way he thinks about you. The better the information packed into those questions, the more likely the arrogance will fade in recognition of your superior response.

Oftentimes a person's source is herself and her own set of rules. Your best bet is to offer new information, evidence, and sources with confidence. Remember, you are talking to a person who has every right to her own rules, just as you have every right to yours—but this does not make her the supreme authority on anything. You can challenge her status quo by suggesting a new perspective. "Well, then, here's an idea. You don't 'do' the public speaking thing, and I get that. But you're the most knowledge- able person in the department on these new findings—you're the one always reading the trades, right? We really need you to get the rest of us up to speed. If you make the slides, I'll present them. How's that?"

When the Clicking Gets Tough . . .

Stumbling blocks can cause a lot of frustration, and removing the stumbling block may require patience, flexibility, and deter- mination. The good thing about running into one is that once you know you've hit something, you can identify and eliminate it. Even when communication is difficult, slow going, or antago- nistic, you can resolve the issues that stand between you and another person and make that click.

CHAPTER 13

Group Click

MOST PEOPLE WANT TO BE PART OF SOMETHING GREATER than themselves. But people are independent by nature, so to harness the raw power of the individual and get it to work in the service of a greater good, you need to not only get everyone together but also get them to "get" each other. You need to bring people together around an idea or mission. You need a group click.

Inspiring a group of people doesn't mean convincing everyone to have the same point of view. The benefits of creating a group click are powerful and give you a way to move mountains. With group click, you'll begin to see heightened levels of connection, cooperation, productivity, teamwork, clear communication, and ultimately less stress.

A really good group click ultimately happens from the group itself, not just one member of the group.

While you essentially want to inspire a group to click together, it may take one member to get the ball rolling on a group click, and sometimes to ensure that it keeps rolling in the right direction. That person can be you. Follow the five strategies below to ensure that your group can click together.

1. Hold the focus.

To create a sustainable group, you need to give people a good reason to come together and stay together. And you need to give them a way to act on that good reason. Keep people connected by regularly reminding them that "This is what we're doing, why we're doing it, and why it matters."

A good reason tells people not just what the group does— what they, as part of the group, do—but also *why* they do it. And why it matters. A good reason creates shared purpose and meaning, and lets people know both *that* they are contributing to the greater good and *how,* exactly, they can do so.

Identify the reason, then hold the focus on it. This gives everyone something in common. Create a central idea that will attract people to it, then keep it in front of people so that they will concentrate their attention on it.

It's like the old story of a guy walking down the street, past three bricklayers at work on a church. The guy asks the first one, "What are you doing?" and the bricklayer replies, "I'm laying bricks." The guy asks the second one, "What are you doing?" and the bricklayer replies, "I'm laying bricks to build a wall." The guy asks the third one, "What are you doing?" and the bricklayer replies, "I'm building a sanctuary." (Which one would you hire to work on your home?) To help a group click, invite them to build a sanctuary, not just lay some bricks.

2. Identify a positive common goal.

To get a group to click and keep them clicking together, give them a shared goal as a rallying point. Provide a clear target for them to aim at (and clear ways to hit it).

The first step is to identify your common goal. Make it something positive—that's more likely to bring out the best in people. Positive association allows for proactive behavior, inventiveness, and creative collaboration. Even in negative situations, a positive vision for the future keeps a group clicking by giving them something to work toward.

Sometimes a negative focus can get a group going. When you play to fears, offer worst-case scenarios, or create or promote a common enemy, you will get people to focus on defeating the bad guy. This can be powerful when a group is truly under siege, successfully rallying them for a fight. But in doing so, they may suspend their creative and reasoning abilities in favor of hyper-fixation on the villain. Ultimately, that will never sustain a click.

People do come together in a crisis, as we see in the outpouring of support for the victims of hurricanes, terror attacks, earthquakes, and the like. Still, the best and most long-lasting efforts are in the service of something positive—moving toward something better, not just away from something bad. Fear will eventually exhaust itself, but desire is a sustainable motivation. Over the long haul, hope always trumps fear.

3. Treat people with respect.

Treating people with respect sets the stage for them to respect you and your vision, to be able to hear you and your invitations to click with the group. There's no call to value, admire, honor, or revere anyone more than he or she has earned. But you do need to respect everyone as a person doing the best she knows how if you expect to be able to create click. Treating all group members with a basic level of respect means less conflict and more productive engagement.

Everyone wants respect, and no one wants to lose it, but respect means different things to different people. The best advice is to blend, turning the Golden Rule into "Respect others as they would have you respect them."

> The more you know about the way a particular person defines respect, the easier it is to give it—and the easier it is to notice when you receive it.

We all generally recognize respect from others when they don't do to us what they wouldn't want us doing to them, like when they don't make promises they can't keep, or act out emotionally, or embarrass us in front of our peers. The more you know about the way a particular person defines respect, however, the easier it is to give it—and the easier it is to notice when you receive it. One way to know what respect means to someone is to get him talking about people he respects. Another is to notice how he treats people he respects, and then treat him that way. You can also tell him you want his respect, and ask him how you will know you have it.

Respecting group members can take different forms: keeping your distance while they do their work; only offering assistance when it is clearly called for; offering praise and encouragement; talking them up to others. Equally important is to avoid obvious signs of disrespect, like looking away while speaking, talking down, and dismissing comments or ideas as worthless. You can't ignore, degrade, or discount someone (or their needs or values), especially in front of their peers, and expect them to click with anyone, least of all you or your ideas.

4. Invite members' contributions.

To get a group of people to click with one another, seek out ways to increase each one's participation in the group. People are more likely to participate in a group when they feel they are valued members of the group and they know that they are welcome to be themselves, think for themselves, and speak for themselves. One of the best ways to support full participation by implicitly addressing all of these things is to invite people to contribute information and ideas—and to welcome that input when it comes. With this kind of open exchange of ideas and information, group members who have had the chance to personally make a difference in the process feel invested in the group's results.

> Invite people to contribute information and ideas—
> and welcome that input when it comes.

Most people have learned to discount their own ideas, usually as a defense mechanism against having them discounted by others. They fear that speaking up will only get them shot down. Or they anticipate the pattern German philosopher Arthur Schopenhauer put this way: "All truth passes through three stages: First it is ridiculed. Second it is violently opposed. Third it is accepted as being self-evident." Who wants to go through that?

So if you want people to contribute their ideas, how you handle those contributions is key. There's a simple three-step process you can use to greet any idea with openness and respect, thereby encouraging continued participation:

- First, say what you like about it. "Scrap the annual conference this year in favor of a video conference? That strikes me as something that could save a lot of money, not to mention all the time and effort that goes into planning it."

- Second, explain what you don't like about it. "I'm worried, though, about whether we could really make the same connections if we don't meet in person."

- Third (and finally), reveal what makes the idea interesting to you. "Here's what intrigues me: Would attendance decrease with the lack of a central physical location—or increase once the necessity for travel was eliminated? So, hey, interesting idea, thanks for bringing it up!"

This approach is especially useful in addressing an idea you fundamentally disagree with.

Listening in this way invites people to keep speaking up by engaging them and showing that their idea has intrinsic worth.

5. Keep people in the loop.

To keep a group clicking, people need some perspective about the process they are engaged in. What's going on? Where are they now?

So spread the word. Let everyone know about positive results, resources available, resources required, and lessons learned from mistakes made. Share information so everyone can benefit. All of us are smarter than any of us.

To successfully click, groups also need advance notice about change, with enough time to consider it and put in their two cents as necessary. They need to know they have a say. That doesn't mean they get their *way*. But they do need a chance to weigh in. Not about every last thing, or at every single step, but at key places and turning points, you need to keep everyone in the loop.

When you've got something coming down the pike, give your group a chance to click around it. You do this by asking group members for three things:

1. To think about it.
2. To discuss it with one another.
3. To contribute their thoughts and ideas.

This creates a flow of ideas that can not only produce a click but also help you clarify your own thoughts and perhaps make better, or at the very least more informed, decisions. An open process like this also sends a message of respect for the group. And it makes it more likely the group will be ready to buy into the final result, whatever it may be.

· Roadblocks to Group Click

Inviting people to come together and apply their skill and ability to a common purpose is, unfortunately, not always quite enough on its own to bring people together. When a group needs a little something extra to get it to click, the two most common obstacles that must be overcome are force of habit and cynicism.

Force of Habit

If a group is not clicking, it may simply be that they've developed the habit of not clicking. Or, it could be that particular habits of the group are blocking the click—like how they run their meetings, or their process for bringing new ideas to the fore, or the ways people come and go from the group. The group might be operating in ways that keep members from clicking together, interfering with their ability to notice good ideas or new opportunities. Sometimes groups cling to unproductive habits even when they are aware they are less than ideal: It is force of habit that drives people to choose "the devil you know" over "the devil you don't."

In any case, developing new habits will be essential for clicking. Change old habits by creating new ones. Habits take hold through repetition and intensity.

We tend to acquire new habits in the pursuit of a higher purpose. We learn new things, adopt new ideas, and become better at old things when we have a good reason to. So, to move a group in a new direction, begin with the end in mind. What common purpose do the group members share? What puts everyone in the same boat of needing to change? Rather than making a habit of pointing out old habits (and thus reinforcing them), you begin a new habit by finding the tie that binds, and working forward from there. When you have that point of focus, you can keep it in front of people, tie conversations back to it, and remind people of it in every learning opportunity.

Cynicism

Cynicism presents an even bigger challenge to group click. Particularly cynicism about clicking itself. If the attitude is, we haven't clicked before, we're not going to click now, well . . . that is a self-fulfilling prophecy. The cynics who are certain nothing can possibly change will use that to justify contributing nothing of value themselves. Cynics find fault and use it to limit others' good faith efforts. Cynics reflexively scorn the motives of others, which is obviously not conducive to clicking.

Clearing the Roadblocks

To get past these obstacles, all you need are three basic strategies:

1. Be consistent.

Be sure the messages you send out are straightforward and consistent with each other and with your actions. Your habits must match your values, and your words must match your deeds. You need to live by the rules you set. And you need to embody the ideas and values you want the group to click around.

> Your messages need to be straightforward and consistent with each other and with your actions.

And straighten out mixed messages as soon as you become aware of them. Don't just hope they'll go away! You need to address them in as straightforward a fashion as you would anything else.

Mixed messages confuse people, and when they are confused, they become polarized and angry, or they collapse into silence and helplessness. And they become cynical. The clicking stops.

The most common types of mixed messages are: You say one thing and do another, or you insist one thing will happen, while any observer can see something else entirely taking place. Mixed messages might be sent simultaneously (someone nodding yes while saying no) or sequentially (saying the company values its employees on Monday and shifting jobs overseas on Tuesday). Either way, in the resulting confusion, our ability to buy into a shared focus falls by the wayside. You can't talk to the group about the importance of cutting costs then show up with a new laptop. Or exhort everyone to think outside the box yet meet every new idea with "That's not how we do things."

To clear the air when its been fouled by mixed messages, you need to notice the mixed messages, point them out, and then straighten them out. Watch for the confusion or cynicism mixed messages trigger, so you can step in and address them. If something makes little sense and you're the source of it, call attention to it quickly, to prevent conflicting signals from messing with people's minds. If someone else is the source of it, assume good intent and then straighten out the mixed messages by separating the different messages verbally and then asking how they're connected. "You say you want to come at this a new way. But you keep referencing the old way of doing it. Help me understand how these two ideas are related."

And make at least one of your messages that if people around you notice any evidence of cynicism, they can help everyone out by drawing some attention to it and asking about it.

2. Destroy walls.
To get a group clicking again after it's hit a roadblock, you need to eliminate any barrier to success—and brainstorm with the group about how to do so.

Without the necessary knowledge and resources, people in groups won't be able to click properly. And if they don't have what they need already, they need to know where to find it. Sometimes, that knowledge or those resources are on the other side of a wall—and nobody looks there because they can't see them. To facilitate the click, get your group access to whatever it needs—tear down any walls that stand in the way of progress. Remove any barriers between the group and whatever it needs to work. Clear the way for people to do what they know needs to be done.

To get things going again, first you need to identify the wall. You can tell when people are up against a wall because they stop going forward. They can't get what they need. They focus on territory rather than a plan or purpose.

Now you can remove the wall you've found. The way to do that is to engage the people around the wall in finding a new way forward. The magic words are, "How can I help you get past this?" and "What will work better?" Keep the focus on replacing the wall with something helpful, rather than dwelling on the existence of the wall.

Twenty years ago, a Hewlett-Packard manager explained to me his company's main approach for tearing down walls: "Whenever someone makes an excuse, we do what we can to eliminate the source of it." If somebody said, "I don't like my hours," HP would respond with "What hours would you prefer?" If someone said, "I don't like this project," HP would ask "What project would you rather work on?" If someone said he didn't like working with his team, HP would find out who he would rather work with. With all excuses removed, there was no reason not to perform at the highest level.

3. Build bridges.

Sometimes tearing down the walls won't be quite enough: You'll have to build a bridge so the group can get from where it is to where it needs to go. Bridges to get to resources, bridges to get resources to the group, bridges so people can reach one another . . . You can help put everything they need to succeed within their reach.

That kind of involvement and engagement in providing resources goes a long way toward building the connective tissue of a group. And it comes down to asking, listening, and taking action. Sometimes, the best question to ask is "What do you suggest?" If many are involved, collect and collate all the responses in order to identify the missing resources and how best to access them.

Most often, bridge-building is a matter of using your network to share resources and information. The messages you need to send are "You are not alone," "We are in this together," "All of us are smarter and better together than when we are on our own." The sum of the collective resources is always greater than what any one person has access to apart from the group.

Give the People What They Want

You can facilitate a group click by keeping the group focused on what they are doing and why. A clear common goal—for best results, a positive one—gives everyone a rallying point. Speaking and behaving consistently, and treating people with respect—including inviting everyone's contributions and keeping everyone in the loop—gives you the standing to get everyone pulling together. And to get them clicking again after they've hit a roadblock. They'll thank you for it. Left to their own devices, humans tend to act as individuals, first and foremost. But deep down inside, most people really want to participate with others, to engage in something larger than themselves. They want the group click.

CHAPTER 14

Why We Click

I'VE BEEN TEACHING COMMUNICATION AND RELATION-ship skills for three decades and all of my work is based on the idea that if people are going to get along with each other and get things done together, they first have to click. In this book, we've explored what it means to click: How to get people, how to get them to get you, how to get them to get your ideas, and even how to get them to get together.

Most of what's good and worthwhile in life begins with a click. People need each other for their work to be satisfying, for their careers to advance, for their lives to have meaning. Getting along with people is fundamental to anyone's happiness and success. The person who doesn't know how to get along with people is going to have a tremendous amount of trouble getting along in life.

It often seems clicking simply happens, but as this book shows, you don't have to rely on fate, circumstance, or natural chemistry to connect with someone. It may take determination and skill, but knowing how to click means you have the right tools to work better with others, develop stronger teams, and have a higher quality exchange of ideas and information. You can connect with anyone.

Human beings are social by nature. All business is, ultimately, people business. It's time to step out of your familiar behavior and practice what you've learned. It's not just right for you, it's something good you can do in service to all of us. So take all of this information out into the world and start clicking with more people, at home, at work, and in the community of people that surrounds you. The more you try to click with others, the better you'll understand the tools and ideas presented here, and the more people will click with you. Confidence comes from preparation, and being effective is the result of practice. It's not enough to know what to do. You've got to *do* what you know to do in order to master it.

What exactly you do from here—how exactly you use click—is entirely up to you. You can work better with others and get better results. You can develop stronger partnerships and teams. You can have a higher quality exchange of ideas and information, resolve interpersonal problems, and play a bigger part in what goes on around you. Best of all, you can start and build relationships that become real friendships, the kind that last a lifetime.

All change for the better has to start somewhere. Let your change start right here.

Click!